How to Open & a Financially Successful Small Farm

With Companion CD-ROM

Melissa Nelson and Julie Fryer

HOW TO OPEN & OPERATE A FINANCIALLY SUCCESSFUL SMALL FARM: WITH COMPANION CD-ROM

Library of Congress Cataloging-in-Publication Data

Nelson, Melissa G. (Melissa Gwyn), 1969-
  How to open & operate a financially successful small farm : with companion CD-ROM / by: Melissa G. Nelson.
    p. cm.
  Includes bibliographical references and index.
  ISBN-13: 978-1-60138-330-3 (alk. paper)
  ISBN-10: 1-60138-330-4 (alk. paper)
1. Farm management. 2. Farms, Small. I. Title. II. Title: How to open and operate a financially successful small farm.
  S561.N38 2013
  630.68--dc22
                            2010031775

INTERIOR LAYOUT: Antoinette D'Amore • addesign@videotron.ca
COVER DESIGNS: Jackie Miller • millerjackiej@gmail.com

Printed on Recycled Paper

A few years back we lost our beloved pet dog Bear, who was not only our best and dearest friend but also the "Vice President of Sunshine" here at Atlantic Publishing. He did not receive a salary but worked tirelessly 24 hours a day to please his parents.

Bear was a rescue dog who turned around and showered myself, my wife, Sherri, his grandparents Jean, Bob, and Nancy, and every person and animal he met (well, maybe not rabbits) with friendship and love. He made a lot of people smile every day.

We wanted you to know a portion of the profits of this book will be donated in Bear's memory to local animal shelters, parks, conservation organizations, and other individuals and nonprofit organizations in need of assistance.

– *Douglas & Sherri Brown*

PS: We have since adopted two more rescue dogs: first Scout, and the following year, Ginger. They were both mixed golden retrievers who needed a home.

Want to help animals and the world? Here are a dozen easy suggestions you and your family can implement today:

- *Adopt and rescue a pet from a local shelter.*
- *Support local and no-kill animal shelters.*
- *Plant a tree to honor someone you love.*
- *Be a developer — put up some birdhouses.*
- *Buy live, potted Christmas trees and replant them.*
- *Make sure you spend time with your animals each day.*
- *Save natural resources by recycling and buying recycled products.*
- *Drink tap water, or filter your own water at home.*
- *Whenever possible, limit your use of or do not use pesticides.*
- *If you eat seafood, make sustainable choices.*
- *Support your local farmers market.*
- *Get outside. Visit a park, volunteer, walk your dog, or ride your bike.*

Five years ago, Atlantic Publishing signed the Green Press Initiative. These guidelines promote environmentally friendly practices, such as using recycled stock and vegetable-based inks, avoiding waste, choosing energy-efficient resources, and promoting a no-pulping policy. We now use 100-percent recycled stock on all our books. The results: in one year, switching to post-consumer recycled stock saved 24 mature trees, 5,000 gallons of water, the equivalent of the total energy used for one home in a year, and the equivalent of the greenhouse gases from one car driven for a year.

Acknowledgement

Writing a book is usually considered a lonely process, as the writer spends much time alone researching material and writing text. But no writer is an island, and during the creative process, many people contribute to make a book successful. First, I would like to thank those friends and family who supported and encouraged my decision to strike out in writing. I would particularly like to thank Karen Hipple-Perez, who always had a ready ear to listen to my ideas and to help sort through things; Jennifer Hipple, a fellow writer; my sister, Rosanna Callahan; and my brother, Terry Nelson.

I also would like to thank the participants in my case studies who really made the book with their real-life experiences. They were all very open and willing to share their experiences.

Melissa Nelson

Dedication

To my parents, Henry and Suzanne Nelson,
who instilled in me a healthy respect and love
of all creatures great and small.

Melissa Nelson

Table of Contents

Chapter 3: Type of Farm: How Do You Fit In? 55

Chapter 4: Starting Plant Production: Where Do You Begin? 71

Chapter 5: Beginning Animal Production 89

Chapter 6: Researching Your Markets and Selling Your Products 107

Chapter 7: Marketing: How Do I Get the Word Out Effectively? 121

Chapter 8: Setting Up Shop: Planning, Structuring, Licensing, and Insurance 149

Chapter 9: Business Management, Analysis, and Bookkeeping 173

Chapter 10: Government Assistance to Farmers 191

Chapter 11: Loans, Grants, and Investors 213

Chapter 12: The Business Plan...................237

Chapter 13: Maintaining, Growing, or Selling Your Business 247

Introduction

Agriculture in the United States is a large and diversified industry. According to the U.S. Department of Agriculture, there are more than 2.2 million farms in the country today, the majority of which are smaller than 50 acres. Research shows they are more profitable than larger farms; a recent study by Food First, the Institute for Food and Development Policy, found smaller farms (less than 27 acres) are 200 to 1,000 percent more productive than larger farms and generate ten times more profit per acre than their larger counterparts.

Due to its diverse climates and weather, the United States is able to support a farming industry consisting of a wide variety of enterprises. The U.S. also boasts more arable land — land that can support vegetation — than any other country in the world. U.S. farmers bring in approximately $200 billion from both crops and livestock every year. Corn, grown by more than 18 percent of all U.S. farms, is by far the most popular crop. Other major sectors include soybeans, dairy, cattle, poultry, vegetables, and fruit. The U.S. is made up of ten distinct agriculture sections, so divided because of common characteristics relating to soil, climate, slope of land, and the average distance to market. While not an absolute, these regions are better suited to certain agricultural enterprises than others.

U.S. farm production regions

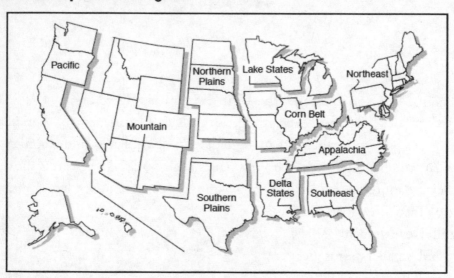

REGION	PRINCIPAL AGRICULTURE
Northeast	Dairy, poultry, fruits, vegetables
Appalachian	Dairy, tobacco, peanuts, beef
Southeast	Fruits, vegetables (both citrus and non-citrus), peanuts, beef, chicken, cotton
Lake States	Dairy, beef
Corn Belt	Corn, Beef, hogs, dairy, feed grains, soybeans, wheat
Delta States	Soybeans, cotton, rice, sugarcane, poultry, livestock

REGION	PRINCIPAL AGRICULTURE
Northern Plains	Wheat, hay, beef
Southern Plains	Wheat, cotton
Mountain	Beef, lamb, wheat, hay, sugar beets, potatoes, fruits, vegetables
Pacific	Wheat, fruit, potatoes, vegetables, cotton, beef, sugarcane, dairy

Farming is an exciting and rewarding career choice. It offers many rewards, many of which are intangible. It truly is a lifestyle. If you are one of the many who have been toying with the idea of starting a small farm, you have come to the right place. Farming is not an easy career to start; there will be hard times. In order to be a successful farmer, two things are required — a love of the earth (as in working with its soil and caring for its animals) and good business practices.

Farming is one of the oldest and most important industries in the world, and it is a wonderful opportunity for what many would call a better life. You get to work for yourself, live in a rural area, and be close to nature. Farming is, first and foremost, a business. In order to be successful in the

industry, you will have to manage it as such. This means choosing what you will grow or raise based on the demand for a product and how much money you can sell it for. It also means keeping an eye on the bottom line and paying attention to where your money goes. This book was created to guide you through things you must consider in starting your own farming business, provide information to help you plan what to grow or raise, and introduce a variety of methods you can employ to help your small farm become a success.

The following pages are filled with information, advice, ideas, plans, sample documents, and resources. This book is meant to be an idea starter and a blueprint for making those ideas a reality. The chapters are not in order of operation or importance — most of the time you will be juggling elements from every chapter at once. The book will touch on every aspect of farming from tilling land to raising chickens to creating a marketing plan to working with your government agencies. Read each chapter, explore all the options, and get your priorities in order before embarking on your business.

Remember that each of these endeavors is a full-fledged discipline of its own and could not possibly be covered fully within one book. However, you do not need to be an expert to incorporate these best practices into your business. After all, as a small business owner of any kind, you must learn to wear all the hats and run all departments. Luckily, numerous resources are available to you to further your education. Once you have narrowed down your idea and as you work through the business process, visit your local library or bookstore for more information on any of these topics. Check online sites dedicated to that field and join trade groups in your area to learn more. The most important thing to remember as you read this book and formulate your own success story is that if you truly want to succeed, you will discover a path to reach your goal.

Happy farming!

Chapter 1

Assess Yourself:
Are You Ready for This?

O wning and operating your own farm business is an exciting prospect. As with any business, it is important to do your homework. Aside from all the decisions you must make, you also need to ask yourself if you are truly ready for such an undertaking. It is one thing to want to work the earth; it is quite another to turn this desire into a career.

Farmers as Entrepreneurs

- Farmers are the original entrepreneurs. Defined as someone who generates profit by capitalizing on opportunities, entrepreneurs have several common traits. While there is no concrete recipe for success, many of these successful business people have certain common qualities. How do your entrepreneurial skills measure up? Review the following list to discover the attributes you share with successful entrepreneurs. Confidence. Farming is an up and down sort of business; some years are great, and other years have you borrowing from piggy banks. You really have to believe in yourself, your farm, and the business of both in order to weather those times. Confidence is also important to a dynamic business such as farming because you frequently have to make decisions and stick by them, such as what to plant that year.

- **Persistence.** Farming is not a business where you can expect to show a profit in the first year. In fact, many people estimate that a new farmer really cannot expect to turn a profit any sooner than five years down the line. You need to have the persistence to get through the lean times. While confidence is a large part of that, when time and circumstances erode the bravado of confidence, persistence is what sees you to the finish line.

- **Focus.** As your own boss, you are responsible for achieving your own success. You continually have to keep your focus on the attainment of your goals. This means working when you do not feel like it, knowing what to spend money on, and realizing what you can do without. In order to be successful in farming, you have to keep your eye on the prize.

- **Ability to innovate.** Farming is a dynamic business; not only does the weather create a changing and unpredictable environment, but the consumer market is also distinctly faddish.

Consider that when low-carbohydrate diets were in vogue, per capita potato consumption dropped more than 10 percent in less than one year, from 145 to 130 pounds per year, and 40 percent of Americans stopped eating bread. If you were a potato farmer at that time, you would have had to use innovative methods to overcome the deficit.

- **Ability to take risks.** Farming is a risky business by nature. A variety of factors — such as weather, insects, disease, and consumer trends — are outside your control but affect your chances of success nonetheless. To be successful, you must be willing and able to accept a certain amount of risk.

- **Leadership abilities.** Farming requires leadership abilities because with a farm, particularly a small one, you stand alone. It is your responsibility to assemble your resources, be it a spouse's accounting ability, the help of a neighbor when you need it, a good deal with your suppliers, or the support of your community.

- **Organization skills.** Farming requires a series of essential chores and tasks that must be completed within the day. To succeed, you must to be able to identify and prioritize these tasks and be organized enough to complete them on time. You also will have to deal with the "mini-crises" that spring up while still getting daily chores done.

- **Long-term view.** The daily demands of farming often mean that long-term planning gets lost in the shuffle. To succeed as a small farmer you must set aside time to plan the future of your farm and put in the additional effort required to make those plans happen.

OK, how are you doing so far?

Farmers as Business Managers

In addition to the entrepreneurial skills, you also need to have managerial skills. The entrepreneur is a creator; he or she sees the opportunity, assembles the resources, and sets a course of action. In contrast, a manager continues the plan; his or her concern is the day-to-day aspects of the business once it is up and running. Managers in all business sectors are skilled in these important areas:

- **Knowing the industry.** A successful business manager has to monitor trends in the economy, technology advancements pertaining to equipment and communications or marketing; government and legal regulations, and competitors and consumer trends that may develop into challenges or opportunities in the future. The farmer is no different. You have to make it your priority to stay current with industry changes.

- **Understanding the basics of business management.** Too many farms fail because of improper business practices. You need to understand all aspects of your business, including bookkeeping, legal issues to watch out for, marketing planning, and planning for getting your product to market. While your purchase of this book is a great first step, consider taking a class or getting a mentor to refine your skills in these areas.

- **Adequate startup capital.** Many businesses fail because they try to start with too little capital to fund everything needed to create a business. You certainly can start on a shoestring;

the trick is working with that shoestring budget to meet all the particulars of starting your business.

- **Managing finances.** Farmers have to be able to manage cash flow effectively to ensure the availability of funds for expenses, supplies, catastrophes, improvements, and growth. As a farmer, your cash flow is likely to be highly volatile. Your ability to manage your finances well in all situations can make or break your farm.

- **Managing time and resources efficiently.** Just as the entrepreneur needs to manage his time, priorities, emergencies, and the involvement of those around him, so too does the business manager. In order to run your farm effectively and profitably in the long term, you first have to manage your time and resources effectively and profitably.

- **Attention to quality.** As a small farmer, you likely will be competing on quality, not price. You will need to make certain that all of your product offerings, from tomatoes to spring calves, are of the highest quality that you can provide. You also will need to ensure that your interactions with customers, wholesalers, and suppliers are of the highest quality.

- **Knowing how to compete.** The minute you attempt to sell something, you have entered the wonderful world of competition; as a farmer, you need to know how to compete. You need to understand how a competitor affects your business, that alternate products exist and act as competition as well, how to market your products effectively, and how to select the best venues for sales.

- **Coping with regulations and paperwork.** While all businesses require some level of paperwork and regulations, farmers have additional considerations because lives are concerned — the lives of your animals as well as the lives of your consumers. You will need to deal occasionally with large amounts of regulations, paperwork, and mandatory record keeping and inspections.

As you can see, to ensure a smoothly operating and profitable farm, the small farmer needs to wear many hats. Even with the best planning and management, many things can go wrong. Considering these factors up front will help you decide if small farming is really for you.

```
CASE STUDY:
KNOW THY FARM -
A DIFFERENT
BUSINESS MODEL
```

Jan Hoadley
http://slowmoneyfarm.com

Jan Hoadley is the visionary behind Slow Money Farm, a community-sponsored agriculture (CSA) enterprise. Farming is in her blood. She grew up on a family farm that raised purebred Charolais cattle. She also had experience with horses, Brown Swiss cattle, and pigs. Tiring of the urban life, Hoadley decided to venture into agriculture through the development of Slow Money Farm.

Slow Money Farm operates a bit different from other CSA farms. While they will do offer their customers subscriptions for products, they plan to emphasize the use of rare animal breeds and heirloom vegetables to help preserve these endangered species from extinction. However, since Slow Money is a business, each animal will have to pay for itself by producing meat, fiber, or milk in large enough quantities to be financially sustainable.

Currently, Slow Money Farms raises several animal breeds that are on the American Livestock Breeds Conservancy endangered list. These include American Chinchilla and Giant Chinchilla rabbits along with Dominique, Silver Laced Wyandotte, Plymouth Rock, and Black Australorp chickens. Most of these breeds have become endangered as they have characteristics that make them unsuited for modern confinement systems. As they expand, they plan to include other animal species such as ducks, geese, turkeys, goats, cattle, donkeys, and horses.

Heirloom vegetables also "pay" for themselves as seeds from these varieties are saved to be planted next year. This is unlike hybrid breed vegetables in which the seeds from the hybrid vegetable generally are not good for planting.

Slow Money Farm plans to custom raise animals and vegetables for a small number of people who will pay a fee to help secure land and the needed supplies to produce the final product. Products will be delivered off site at a prearranged location. Milk is not marketed from the farm due to state regulations but it is "marketed" by using it as food for pigs, chickens, or bottle calves. Giant Chinchilla and American Chinchilla rabbits are also raised for show and for breed preservation. Those rabbits that do not make the cut for show or breeders are used for meat-market animals.

By keeping the number of customers small (fewer than 20), Slow Money Farm will keep foot traffic to the farm low, an important aspect of biosecurity. Fewer farm visitors means less chance of disease transmission. One method Slow Money Farm plans to use to keep their clients involved in the farm is through the use of webcams and video "vlogs" from the farm to let the clients visually see how the animals are raised and to keep updated on the farm.

Slow Money Farm will connect with customers and others through extensive use of social media sites such as Facebook® and Twitter®. Due to the wide variety of products raised on the farm, recipes will also be shared via these sites to help customers get the most from each product. Social media sites are also useful tools for breed promotion, photos, general farm information, and interesting videos.

Slow Money Farm is an exciting concept merging the new (social media) and the old (long-established breeds) into a self-sustaining farm and providing customers with a healthy alternative to supermarket foods.

The Downside

In the excitement of starting a new venture, many would-be business owners make a common mistake when thinking about opening their own business: they forget to consider the potential downside to this new business. Success is about preparation. As you go forward in the pursuit of opening your own small farm, it is important to consider carefully the various issues or problems associated with the type of farm you are planning to run. Neglecting to consider the possible negatives may mean finding yourself unprepared and ill-equipped to handle these issues effectively when they occur.

The following is a list of some of the issues you should consider before opening your own small farm:

- **Uncertainty of income.** Starting a farm requires investment, and the fruits of your labor may not bear for a couple of years. You need to be prepared to live on savings or another source of income until your harvests come in or your farm shows a profit. It will be necessary to tighten the belt for the first few years. Are you ready for that? Is your family ready for that?

- **Risk of losing everything.** There are no guarantees in business; you could lose everything. While careful planning and good research can greatly lower the chances of that happening, your farm still could fail. It is important that you spend some time evaluating this likelihood and develop a course of action to implement in case this does happen.

- **Hard, seasonal work.** As rewarding as it is, farming comes with long hours and seven-day workweeks for most of the growing season. The tasks involved and the hours required vary a great deal depending on the season. Expect to have little time for anything other than your farm during certain times, particularly when you first start out.

- **High stress levels.** Having your own farm is rewarding, but it also can be stressful. Aside from the normal stresses of business — such as competitors, the economy, and consumer trends — you also have the additional stress of worrying about the weather, the uncertainties of livestock health, and even the volatility of the market Take snow, for example; before becoming a farmer, snow was a beautiful act of nature that entitled you and the kids to a snow day. To a farmer, snow means that the taste and texture of your vegetables will change, and your animals might need extra heat.

A high-risk profession

Farming is considered one of the most dangerous jobs in the United States. Hundreds of farmers and ranchers are killed each year, and thousands suffer debilitating injuries that will end their farm careers. For youth farm workers, the risk goes even higher, and it is considered the No. 1 most dangerous job for teens. This is often because kids start working on the family farm at a young age and often are untrained, unsupervised, and impulsive. Beyond the typical bumps, bruises, or breaks, many farm injuries are quite serious such as severed limbs, concussions, or suffocations. Long-term exposure to sun, heat, or loud noises can lead to skin cancer, dehydration, or hearing loss. Even an innocent fun ride on the tractor for your grandchild can turn deadly if the tractor tips or rolls over.

The potential risks on any farm run the gamut from large, heavy equipment to powerful, unpredictable animals to noxious, toxic chemicals. Add to that beginner's inexperience, isolated work conditions, exhausting work schedules, and sudden bad weather, and you can see why farming makes this notorious list. These risks are not to be taken lightly, and it is critical to learn, practice, and teach safe farm practices to all workers, family members, and visitors to your farm. The USDA website has various links related to farm safety tips, youth farm safety classes, and resources to find more information. Check with your local extension office or 4-H club for printed materials or videos to help in your training.

Chapter 2

Resources Required: What Do You Actually Need?

s you commit money and resources to starting your own farm, you will need to choose between what you really need to operate and what you can acquire in the future. Some things will be good investments and worth the extra money, while others warrant caution before proceeding with a purchase. Spending time to research and evaluate potential investments properly will ensure your money is wisely spent on resources that will benefit you immediately and well into the future. Knowing what resources are required, and what are optional, also will help save you money for emergencies and unexpected expenses.

Many new farmers must first focus on buying land or space to raise their crops or animals, and purchasing equipment to get the job done. Without these two critical ingredients, you have no way to raise a crop or grow a herd. Various options do exist, though, that do not cost a lot of money. This chapter will describe your options in these two areas so you can start assembling the resources necessary for your farm.

Equipment

Every farm needs a few tools and pieces of equipment, but before you run down to the implement dealer with your credit card, make a list of what you will truly need. Many times you will find that you use only a few tools for getting your work done. You also can find good used tools and equipment at local auctions, classified ads, or online sites such as Craigslist®. When buying mechanical equipment, though, such as vehicles or tractors, be sure to deal with a reputable dealer or friend who will offer you a warranty. Starting out, there are several essentials:

Tractors

Many people who want to be farmers picture themselves astride a tractor doing farm work. In reality, a tractor simply might not be necessary and could prove to be more cost than reward. Unless you know how to fix and maintain a tractor, you will spend a good amount of money on upkeep. The tractor itself is just a source of power; the real utility is in the attachments. The type of tractor and attachments you need depend on the size and scope of your farm. Visit your local implement dealer to get an idea of what you need to run your operation. You also can price brand new equipment to give you a starting point for cost. Tractors can cost anywhere from $5,000 for a small used tractor in good shape to well over $80,000 for a new utility type tractor.

If you do not plan to buy large farm equipment, you might need to hire a tractor along with someone to operate it. Equipment rental and operator fees range widely by region and the type of chore but you can expect to pay between $30 and $50 per hour for most jobs such as manure spreading, plowing, mowing hay, or general field work. Fees might go higher at busy times of the year such as harvest season.

You often can find small tractor and equipment rentals at machine rental businesses. These tractors can pull small plows or other machinery used for planting pastureland or small fields of crops. Skid steers are also quite versatile and come with many bucket attachments such as hay bale spears for moving large bales. Skid steers do not have the capability of doing field work such as pulling a plow or a planter.

ATVs

One invaluable machine to have on a small-scale farm is an all terrain vehicle (ATV). A mid-sized new ATV can be purchased for around $6,000 and is a good first machine investment for a small scale-farm. Depending on its size, an ATV can pull a harrow to break up manure pats in the pasture or to smooth a recently plowed field. They can pull trailers and small manure spreaders. Front-end attachments are available to enable you to plow snow with an ATV. Driving one around the fence line can save you time when checking pasture fence.

Farm trucks

While a truck or van is great to have on a farm, you can get by with a sturdy car or minivan, especially early on. A van, or car, also has the benefit of allowing you to transport things without worrying about the weather.

Rototillers

You likely will need to have two rototillers: one strong, gear-driven model with around 10 to 12 horsepower, and a smaller, portable rototiller. The rototiller should be able to handle the job in one pass. If your land is rocky or has hard soil, you may need a tractor with a till-ing attachment. Although tilling is vital for keeping weeds at bay and cover crops at statis, tilling less is better for your soil. In addition, many animals' daily activities can help till and cycle the soil. For example, chickens will peck the ground, and pigs will root the soil for bugs and roots.

Trimmers

Buying a good trimmer will save you from the type of repetitive motion like those involved in using hand tools or scythes. These motions can cause joint problems and numbness in your hands and fingers. A gas-powered string trimmer is good for maintaining your property and many trimmers have attachments available to transform a string trimmer into a polesaw or small tiller. Wheeled trimmers have the advantage of reducing strain on your back and shoulders. The choice often simply comes down to personal preference.

Carts and wheelbarrows

You will need a way to move waste, tools, feed, or harvests around your farm and a heavy-duty carts and wheelbarrow can have multiple uses. Be sure to buy a well-made cart, as you usually will be transporting something you do not want spilled or damaged. A good wheelbarrow or yard cart can cost up to $300, but the investment is well worth it, as it should last for years. Make sure to choose a cart that is the right height and weight for you to handle yourself.

Hand tools

From spades to hammers to cordless drills, your farm will require an arsenal of hand tools. Buy the basics to begin with, and add tools later as you find a need. Purchase the highest quality tools you can afford — tools made of hardened steel and with hickory handles usually will last a lifetime. These tools will be the workhorses of your everyday farm life, and you do not want to be without a necessary tool because the handles snapped off. Be sure, too, the tool is the right weight and length for you to handle for long periods.

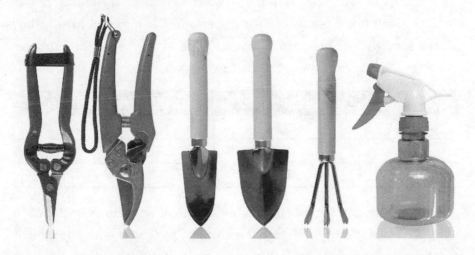

Temporary shelters

If you are planning to start seeds for produce or flowers, you will need at least two temporary shelters, each about 12 feet by 40 feet. These can be made from collapsible materials such as a hoophouse or with movable walls as those used in a greenhouse. Use one as a plant starting area, potting shed, and storage area; use the other for growing high-value crops to protect the crops and extend their growing season. If you plan to raise chickens, you can build a permanent chicken house in the center of the sheltered growing area. Using temporary or movable fencing, the chickens can till and fertilize parts of the area on a rotating basis.

Irrigation equipment

Depending on your region, you may need a permanent irrigation system laid out to reach all of your crops. Many small farms, though, can get by with a system of spouts and hoses spread out throughout the property that you will operate manually when watering is needed. Permanent in-ground or elevated irrigation systems are time-savers, though, as they can be set on timers to water automatically.

To plan for proper hose size, consider how much water you really need for your purpose. If you are only filling a watering can or sprinkling flower plants, you will not need a lot of water at once. It may sound silly, but selecting the right size hose can save you a good bit of money; not only are skinnier hoses less costly, but they also use less water.

Diameter Hose	Gallons per Minute	Minutes to Water 1,000 sq. ft.
1/2"	10.5	63
5/8"	17	37
3/4"	31	24

Whatever system you choose, be sure to lay out all water lines so there is a freeze-proof faucet every 100 feet. This will provide you with convenient access to water anywhere in the field and make it easier to drain the lines before winter. Most systems cost approximately $1 per foot of irrigation line plus the costs of fittings, clamps, faucets, and installation.

Plant supports

Supporting your plants as they grow is important to make sure the fruits closest to the ground receive adequate sunlight, avoid excess moisture, and stay out of reach of ground insects. Staking your plants also will give them room to grow as the season progresses. Supports can range from found materials such as a trellis made of willow branches to store-bought metal tomato cages. Just make sure you have the necessary supports in place before your plants get too big to manage.

Fencing or enclosures

Your fencing needs will vary depending on the crop or animal you are raising. Obviously large animals such as cattle need barns and sturdy fences. Smaller animals are happy in small enclosure that can be moved to grassy areas as needed. A fence around your plants prevents damage from wayward livestock or wild animals. Furthermore, wide grass paths around these areas will provide you with ample room for maneuvering equipment.

Land

Land is the foundation of any successful agricultural venture and choosing land with quality soil and slope is crucial to farming success. *(The characteristics of good land will be covered later in this chapter.)* Not only do you need to consider the land's viability, but you also must review the location as it relates to your needs. These can include: proximity to sales venues or delivery hubs; location of doctors, veterinarians, and suppliers; access to utilities such as Internet; and general accessibility of the property.

Many areas also have unique regulations in place, such as water-use restrictions or property-line setbacks that can affect your ability to raise animals or crops. Check at your local extension office to be sure the property you are considering is not placed in one of these special programs. There also might be government assistance programs in place to help you buy or improve land for farming; ask your extension agent for more information. Property and income taxes also vary by region and by the type of land you are purchasing. Some states are "farmer-friendly" while others do not allow tax breaks for farm land. Review these laws carefully and speak with your accountant before committing to a large land or farmstead purchase.

Leasing or renting

When selecting property for your farm, you first need to determine if you should buy or lease the land. Buying the land will require more money up front, and you will need to stick with farming this land for at least five years. If you decide to quit farming and sell the land too soon, you might not recoup your original purchase expenses. Leasing can be a good option for the beginning farmer as it offers less up-front financial risk or long-term commitment, and it gives you a chance to try out operating your own small farm before buying in all the way. As a small farmer, renting land or barn space works well because you do not need vast tracts of land to meet your goals. You also get the added advantage of access to the landowner who may be a more experienced farmer happy to show you the ropes.

Renting, however, can be expensive as crop prices continue to rise — some Midwestern states recently have seen yearly double-digit percentage increases, and the trend seems to be continuing upward. When you pay for land to farm, you are taking money directly out of your bottom line to pay your landlord. As with all renting arrangements, money paid out in this manner does not help you build equity or pay down a mortgage. Furthermore, with this increased value on rental land, you might have trouble finding land that is available for rent.

Most landowners offering rentals will charge you per acre, however, some are now charging a percentage of the final harvest dollars or requiring a rental commitment of more than one season. Terms will vary greatly by region, and you will need sharp negotiating skills to ensure you get the best deal for your needs. In addition, the landowner can restrict you from planting certain crops if it affects their crop rotation schedules or conservation plans.

Aside from the cost, the biggest disadvantage of leasing is that you will not be living near your land or animals, and you might need additional space to store your equipment and supplies. When you own your own farm, you will have outbuildings to house feed and supplies, and you will have a nearby bed for those all-nighters of harvest or calving. This can be much more convenient during busy times of year or when emergencies such as bad weather occur.

Buying or building

Owning your own farm has a certain intangible quality that only a farmer can appreciate. There is just something incredible about looking out your kitchen window and seeing your crops growing or animals grazing in the pasture. This intangible, though, can be expensive to create from scratch and requires a large amount of up-front cash and a steady income to pay the mortgage, taxes, and upkeep. Compared to renting, though, you will build equity with every improvement and know that all your hard work is going into growing your future. You also have total control over how the farm functions, and you can make changes that fit into your long-term plan. In addition, if you purchase a large farm, you can, in turn, lease un-used land and space out to others.

Unless you have inherited or otherwise own property suitable for a farm, one of the most important questions you must consider is whether to purchase an established farm or build one yourself. Issues are associated with each option.

Advantages of building

When you build your farm from the ground up, you have certain advantages that really can make a difference in your approach to the farming business and in your comfort level:

- You can break into things gradually. When you start from scratch, you have the option to build your farming business gradually, rather than jumping into a full-fledged operation. Even including the purchase of land, many people find that this is an affordable option, as it allows you the freedom to start small and grow into the business, concentrating on successful ventures and leveraging finances and experience as acquired. This method works very well for types of farming that have few barriers to entry or expansion, such as vegetables and beef.

- Starting from scratch also allows you to choose the location for your farm. You get to choose where to live, and you can choose a place close to your future selling venues. You even could identify the perfect spot based on the particular characteristics of the land, such as soil or slope, or a certain feature that strikes you, such as an old tree or a small pond.

- You also have the advantage of arranging the farm in exactly the way you want. Everything will be constructed and laid out according to your specifications and vision. You also can build your farm with energy efficiency and modern farm practices in mind — something you will not find in older farms.

Advantages of buying

Of course, buying an existing farm has its own advantages:

- It already has an established customer base, which translates to cash flow. Additionally, the existing farm probably has built-in relationships with suppliers and distributors of which you could take advantage. Some existing farms even will have the benefit of a reputable brand associated with the farm. Altogether, these factors can improve your odds of success, especially if you can get some tips from the previous owner.

- It also can be considerably cheaper to buy an existing farm because everything is used and frequently reduced further than resale cost to help ensure a turnkey sale. This means that everything you need to get started is included, from the buildings to the equipment.

If this is an option for you, spend time investigating the farm. Ask yourself these questions:

- **What is the farm's history and why is it being sold?** It may just be that the previous owner has passed away, and the family no longer wants to farm. Conversely, the current owner might just be in over his head and is not doing well as a farmer. In either case, it is important to know the background of the seller. If the farm has not been properly maintained or managed, you might end up with more problems than you bargained for.

- **What is the financial condition?** Make sure that you get financial statements from the farmer for at least the last three years, preferably five years. As with any business, a potential investor would not put money into a company without seeing a complete business plan, including its financial history? The key here is to look for trends in costs, sales, and profit margins.

- **What assets are included?** While starting with some of the previous farmers' assets can be a good idea cost-wise, it may be that you would rather purchase new equipment, would rather build a new house, or intend to run a different type of farm than the previous owner. This is typically a negotiable point, and it could save you a good bit of money.

- **What is the condition of the assets?** Make sure you take a good look at any assets that are to be included in the sale, and bring along a professional if you are unsure of how to assess condition. Recognizing proper building construction, fence installation, and drainage issues may help you to forestall problems or give you the option to walk away from a potential disaster. A farm building that is poorly maintained will deteriorate rapidly leading to costly repairs or replacement expense. Assets typically include buildings, tools, internal structures, equipment, and livestock. Remember this is a used farm, so things will not be in mint condition — you can, however, expect things to be functioning and well-maintained. If not, determine how much work is needed to repair or replace these items and include this in your offer. Are there personnel on the farm? If there are employees, are they staying? If not, where can you find good labor? More to the point, do you even want to be an employer? Do you have that option with the size of the farm as it stands?

- **What are the conditions of the land and soils?** We will get into the issue of soil characteristics later in this chapter. However, you should ask the previous owner how much of the land is suitable for farming and inquire about the overall condition of the soil. It may be that disease ravaged the fields last year or that the farmer failed to rotate his crops. You will be able to judge certain elements yourself, but you may want to consider having a soil test done or bring an expert.

- **Are there any environmental issues?** Older farms still may be operational but often do not comply with current environmental laws and regulations. This is because the farm was "grandfathered" in, meaning that because the farm existed before the inception of the new regulation, it is exempt from it. You, as a new owner taking over after the enactment of the law, would be responsible for making sure that the farm is brought up to standard.

This is not necessarily a bad thing as you will be helping the environment, but it can be costly to make improvements in this manner. Check with the local extension office for information on regulations in your area.

Once you have these questions answered, you can go on to the next step: deciding upon a fair price for the land and associated assets.

How much should I pay?

Farm processes are calculated using the fair market value (FMV) of the business as a whole. The FMV can be any price that both the buyer and seller agree upon, and it can be calculated in several ways, including market comparison, asset valuation, and income valuation. It is a good idea to use a combination of methods to ensure a fair price. Your realtor, attorney, or accountant can help you calculate these values. If you are serious about a particular property, consider hiring a professional appraiser to work up a value — this professional appraisal most likely will be necessary anyway if you are pursuing financing.

Farm market comparison

This evaluation method fares well in established markets with a steady number of recent sales. It also might show a large amount of properties that have not sold or have sat on the market for a long time. This can indicate a low overall value, which can be a boon to the buyer but a problem if you are planning to sell in the near future. The results of this research can help you find undervalued properties or steer you away from those that are priced too high.

When creating a market comparison, it is important look for farms with similar characteristics to the farm you are considering, including size, age, location, products, and soil condition. Farming businesses carry certain unique elements such as a niche crop or unusual structures that can make it difficult to compare accurately, so be sure you are fairly judging the property based on other sales. Most appraisers will include these statistics in their comparisons.

Asset valuation

Asset valuation is simply a totaling up of all the assets included in the sale, such as the house, the buildings, the land, the animals, and the equipment. This method is fairly straightforward, until the valuation method is considered. Assets may be valued at net book value or estimated market value. If the farm business has a balance sheet prepared by an accountant, the assets already have been valued at net book value. This means that assets are taken at their purchase value and then depreciated for each year of ownership.

For older farms, this means that asset valuation by net book value will result in a number rather different from the FMV. Alternatively, you can calculate the FMV of each asset and total those figures; this method is referred to as asset valuation by estimated market value. Quite simply, assets are looked up in published guides of used farm equipment and land prices, either through a sales magazine or guides published for this purpose.

The drawback to asset valuation is that sometimes the sum of the parts is greater than the whole. For example, the owner may have upgraded his milking system to a state-of-the-art, expensive system but it is still housed in an old barn. The old barn needs enough work that it essentially eats away at the value of the new system. Breaking value down bit-by-bit can be a tedious process which in the end creates a negotiating hassle. It is a good tool to find a ballpark figure, but ultimately, you are buying the whole farm not its individual parts.

Income valuation

Last, you can value the farm based on its earning potential, or how much income the farm potentially can generate. This can be more complicated to do, and it may be best left to a professional financial analyst. The idea of income valuation is based on the premise that a business earns money based on its current assets. This calculation requires that future cash flows be estimated using the current value of money and then discounted to present value by the amount of interest you could earn in the same period if investing in something stable, such as putting the money in an interest-bearing savings account.

To calculate the FMV of a farm, determine what the forecasted cash flows are expected to be over the life of the farm, treating any investments you may make as negative cash flow. Next, choose your discount rate — usually the current value of a ten-year government bond or the rate you can get for a savings account or CD at your local bank. Then use the following formula to determine the FMV:

$$FMV = C_0 + [C_t / ((1+r)^t)]$$

C_0 is the cost

C_t is the cash flow expected in a period (i.e. yearly), minus investments

r is the discount rate (the interest of the safe investment)

t is the time period (i.e. first year, second year)

This is a useful tool to evaluate a business because it factors in the time value of money. The value of one dollar today is much different from the value of a dollar tomorrow. Investing that dollar today will earn interest but inflation can make that interest disappear. Putting your money into less liquid accounts also means you might not have enough access to your funds, which could lead to additional debt and its interest, overdraft fees, or negative supplier relationships.

The main drawback with this method is that it is subjective because you must assume things such as future investments. This method also assumes that conditions will remain stable — such as interest rates staying consistent — and stability is simply not a part of some transactions, such as an adjustable-rate mortgage. Additionally, the uncertainty and volatility of the farm market in many cases cannot be forecast. As such, perform the calculation using different discount rates to see how much the value of the transaction can differ.

Location

Location is paramount when selecting the property for your farm. You will need to be close enough to your chosen sales venues in order to exploit the opportunities afforded by farmers' markets, subscription services, and wholesale distributors. You likely will be looking for property that is secluded but still only a short 30 minutes from town. If possible, consider looking in the area between two towns so you have potential markets in both directions. Even if you are only going to pursue one as a selling venue, easy accessibility to another town provides options for the future or a place to unload a heavy surplus of your products.

Proximity to a well-appointed town or city also may be a consideration, as not all rural areas are equipped with the amenities and supplies your farm might need. Farm life does require a lot of driving into town; if that town houses a good vet, a family doctor, a building or farm supply store, and a grocery store, your life will be easier. Also, consider your family needs, such as a school, social opportunities, a place of worship, and other amenities you might be used to as a city dweller.

Utilities and alternative energy

You also should ask about the available utilities, such as electricity, natural gas, television services, telephone, and Internet services. Sometimes utility lines already may be present on the land, or it might be necessary to pay to

have the lines run to the property. Furthermore, in some rural areas, water and sewer is provided through systems of wells, cisterns, and septic tanks and may not be serviced by a municipal line. Your real estate agent can provide you with information specific to any property you are considering.

In cases where utilities do not go to the land, or if you simply prefer not to use traditional utilities, you might be interested in a practice called homesteading or going off the grid. Homesteading refers to generating your own electricity, pumping water from a well, burning wood for heat, and so on instead of receiving these services from a utility company. With alternative energy sources receiving more and more attention nationwide, the possibility of going off the grid is becoming more real. The price of adopting such technology is lowering which makes homesteading a more affordable reality. Solar panels, hydrogen fuel cells, and wind turbines can provide all the electricity a home needs, even accommodating satellite communications for telephone, television, or Internet capabilities.

Whether using alternative energy will be an option for your small farm will depend on a variety of factors, such as how much solar energy can be generated by the amount of exposure your home has, how much wind you get, and whether you have a running stream on your property. If you are considering going off the grid, consult your real estate agent and an alternative energy expert in order to ensure that all available options are weighed appropriately and costs evaluated. These technologies often have a large up-front cost but typically pay for themselves within a few years — in some cases, you even can sell the generated electricity back to the utility company.

Whether using alternative energy will be an option for your small farm depends on a large variety of factors including:

- **Capital costs.** Some forms of alternative energy, wind turbines for example, are still new technology and are likely to be expensive.

- **Operating costs.** A common misperception regarding alternative energy is that it is free; it is not. There are operation and maintenance costs that you must consider when deciding if alternative energy is right for you and your farm.

- **Efficiency.** Not all forms of alternative energy are made equal; some are inefficient in comparison to other forms of energy. You will need to weigh how much the energy produced by one form of alternative energy will compare to other forms of energy.

- **Is it renewable?** Wind and solar are considered renewable energy sources and do not require additional fuel or time to process. If you are using resources such as wood or corn pellets to produce heat, though, you are not using a renewable resource. Weigh the costs and environmental impacts of these methods again the energy produced. Is it dependable? For example, the energy produced by a wind turbine is erratic. If that was your sole source of electricity, some days you would have plenty; other days, none at all. If you are running a farm that requires heat or light, you will need a backup generator.

- **Energy production and storage requirements.** Different types of alternative energy have different capacities as to what they can produce and how much of that energy can be stored. Your farm may require a large amount of energy and some types of alternative energy are not conducive to this level of production.

- **Pollution.** Some forms of alternative energy have their own inherent pollution, such as the smoke generated by a wood-burning stove.

- **Environmental modification.** Alternative energy often requires physical modifications of existing structures to deliver a reliable source of energy adequately, such as digging a large trench for geothermal pipes.

Comparative costs of alternative energy

Evaluation	Solar Thermal	PV	Hydro	Wind	OTEC	Tidal	GEO
Capital Costs	Large	Large	Enormous	Moderate	Enormous+	Enormous	Small
Operating Costs	Moderate	Moderate	Neglegible	Small	Unknown	Neglegible	Small
Efficiency	15%	5--10%	80%	42%	7% +	25%	100%
Renewable	Yes	Yes	Yes	Erratic	Yes	Yes	NO
Storage	Not Needed	Unclear	Built-IN	Essential	Not Needed	Unclear	Not Needed
Pollution	None Really	Waste Heat	None	Visual	None	None	Steam Plumes
Levelized Costs	25 cents KWH	16 cents KWH	4 cents KWH	4.5 cents KWH	Unknown	Unknown	Low
Environmental Impact	Moderate	Large	Enormous	Small	Unknown	Outrageous	Small
Large Scale	Too Expensive	Possible but Expensive	Proven already	Very Possible	The Solution	Discrete Locations	Discrete Locations
Small Scale	NO	Difficult	Low Head --> Legal	Definitely	NO	NO	NO
Unit Capacity	1000 MW	Depends on Acreage	2000-6000 MW	Highly Variable	As large as you need	250 MW	1000 MW

Taxes

It is important to research all the tax considerations attached to your property and the area you choose to settle in. First, look at the property taxes, which can be a huge expense and one that is not negotiable. Property taxes vary considerably by region and can be payable to your state, city, and county. Portions of your property also might be taxed at different rates according to its use such as land tax versus homestead tax. Talk to your real estate agent or contact the tax assessor's office in the property's county to find out what the property taxes are for at the coming year.

Additionally, many states charge a personal income tax — usually based on a percentage of your income after deductions and expenses. Different states assess different percentages of income tax. Alaska, Florida, Nevada, New Hampshire, South Dakota, Tennessee, Texas, Washington, and Wyoming have no state income taxes, whereas Vermont has a state income tax that can be as high as 9.5 percent; Oregon, Iowa, and New Jersey each have a state income tax of approximately 9 percent. Also, many areas have a sales tax on certain items but usually not necessities such as food. These numbers can vary dramatically, for example, if you live in Wyoming, approximately $7 for every $100 spent goes to the state, but if you live in New Jersey, you will remit $12 for every $100 spent. Remember, though, these increased taxes often translate into more municipal services such as better road conditions or local amenities. Check the website of the state you are considering for more information on tax rates.

Zoning

Zoning is another issue that can affect the operation of your farm negatively. State, county, or city governmental agencies often have rules in place prohibiting animals, farming, or other business activities in certain areas or in proximity to neighboring homes. Be sure to check for zoning requirements on your property as well as neighboring properties. These laws vary considerably by region, so be sure to visit your state's department of agriculture for more information on such laws as they pertain to your special circumstances, or contact the USDA at **www.usda.gov**.

Characteristics of the Land

After you have settled on a general location, next you will need to consider the physical characteristics of the land such as topsoil depth and composition, slope of the areas you will be planting, surrounding wooded areas, and other unique geographical features. These are elements that you will not be able to change significantly and may limit your farming options. In addition to general land characteristics, you also must consider the quality, availability, and consistency of water resources accessible from your land. In some rural areas, water is provided through systems of wells and cisterns and may not be tied to municipal services. This can add extra cost to your operation, as you will be required to maintain existing systems or dig new wells.

Drainage is another important land and water issue. Land with proper slope will allow water to drain and not sit stagnant in one area. This drainage can be used to your advantage if the water is channeled toward vegetable gardens but also can be a hindrance if the liquids do not drain away from livestock pens. Most well-running farms in operation now will have addressed major drainage problems.

Talking to the previous owner of your land can provide insight into the soil and water issues and give you more information on what grows successfully on the plot of land. While your farming interests may be different from those of the previous owner, it can be beneficial to know that a particular field yields good tomatoes or that a certain field tends to get flooded when it rains. Even if the previous owner of the land did not have a farm, perhaps he had a garden or noticed where water collects.

The most important aspect of your land to consider, aside from the ability to build a working farm, is the quality of the soil. Soil will vary in depth, pH, and slope, and the optimum values of depth, pH, and slope will vary by what you want to grow. These characteristics can be amended to accommodate what you are planning to farm, but such remedies are frequently expensive, time-consuming, and often unsuccessful.

Slope

Slope refers to the change in elevation over a specified area and is presented as a percentage. Land that has a slope steeper than 8 percent, meaning that the land has a variation of eight feet in a given 100-foot area, is not suitable for farmland, mainly due to the risk of erosion, and may present limitations for urban development as well. Slope, being the same taken positively or negatively, is always written as a positive number.

The primary issue with slope is the potential for soil erosion. Erosion occurs naturally due to the forces of rain, wind, or other outside forces such as animal traffic. Through these forces the rich topsoil is moved down the slope and redistributed elsewhere. Steeper slopes are more likely to erode and will take away higher quantities of soil. Erosion by water also is increased exponentially by slope length; so longer fields carry greater risk due to the increased velocity of water running down the longer slope. A loss of soil translates to lost crop potential and may cause damage to existing drainage networks as the soil enters the system.

The possibility of erosion and the rate at which it occurs also depends on other factors such as soil characteristics, but slope is a critical make-or-break factor. Excessive slope in the land also can make it hard to move heavy farm equipment such as tractors through the field. While slope can be altered or worked around, this often involves costs that are not feasible for the potential return. *Chapter 4 will talk more about ways to work with slopes and erosion issues.* At this point in your research, look for land without excessive slopes or for land that has already been improved to work with slope issues.

Topsoil depth

The depth of topsoil on your land will determine the types of crops that will grow well and even whether they will grow at all. The topsoil depth refers to how deep the rich, dark layer of soil on top of the earth runs. Underneath topsoil is clay, sand, or rock; many plants do not have root systems that adapt well to these environments. A study performed in 1970 by the Soil Conservation Service, part of the USDA, tested topsoil depths of 5 inches, 12 inches, and 24 inches; respective yields were 158.7 lb/acre, 620.0 lb/acre, and 869.4 lb/acre. As the study indicates, deeper topsoil can help create a better produce yield.

Topsoil depth and quality is fairly consistent throughout each growing region, and you can find more information by checking with your local extension office. Small-scale farmers also can work to improve their existing topsoil with amendments such as mulch, compost, fertilizer, or manure. Many plants do not require a deep layer of topsoil to thrive. Soil depth also will be noted on any seed packets you may purchase. *(Please refer to Appendix B for helpful charts on recommended seed depth and plant spacing.)*

CASE STUDY: THE HAPPY GARDENER

The Happy Gardener
www.thehappygardener.info
877-798-9280

Annette Pelliccio is the founder and CEO of The Happy Gardener. She also specializes in building organic, sustainable farms and CSAs as well as developing organic garden and farm supplies. She started her business in 2003 so she could be at home with her children and work with her favorite pastime, gardening. In 2006, Annette developed an exclusive line of organic products.

Pelliccio is not new to the farming business. She is a third generation gardening business owner and grew up working at the family garden center and landscaping business. The Happy Gardener is a strictly family-run business dedicated to customer service with a wide variety of customers from homeowners to universities and vineyards. Those customers trust that her product is 100 percent safe, effective, and non-damaging to the environment.

The Happy Gardener develops new products based upon listening to clients and researching ways to meet those needs.

She specializes in a number of products, including: organic certified plant foods and fertilizers, organic pest control, organic weed control, cut flower care, root growth developers, soil conditioners, and seed germination products. In addition, her company only uses high performance grains, legumes, and vegetables in their product line. Pellicio's company is set apart from other organic farm suppliers because they use OCIA-certified sea vegetables in all their products to ensure sustainable and environmentally responsible practices. These products contain absolutely no insecticides, pesticides, or herbicides making them so safe that kids, pets, and wildlife can eat them — although that is not suggested. All the products are safe for the environment and waterways and will not contribute to soil or water contamination problems.

Pelliccio's farming experience has led to this wise advice applicable to any farming operation. It is helpful to know what problems (pests, disease, draining, soil conditions) can arise based on specific crop, location, or soil quality beforehand so you can install a prevention program. It is always easier to prevent rather than solve a problem.

The most popular product the Happy Gardener sells is SeaResults Micronutrient Solution. This product is an use-on-anything, organic product that will increase flower, vegetable, and fruit production by up to 47 percent, increase seed germination rate and consistency, and is 100 percent safe for wildlife and the environment. SeaResults Micronutrient Solution is cost effective as one teaspoon makes a gallon of plant food that only needs to be used once a month during the growing season.

The Happy Gardener does have challenges, too, including many misconceptions and a lack of general education in the industry of organics. Clients have to make sure they are working with an organic certified product line. Just because a label reads "natural" or "organic" does not necessarily mean it is true.

Soil quality

Deep topsoil is important but the quality and nutrient value of this soil also must be assessed to determine if it will support good crop quality. Many older farms have depleted soil or poor growing conditions due to overgrowing on one crop or poor drainage. Look for these plant clues when checking the land in areas you will be planting. Again, many of these issues can be corrected, but it is good to know up front what problems you might encounter.

- Quack grass means that your soil is dry or crusty perfect for growing mustard, choys, broccoli, cabbage, or cauliflower.
- Ground ivy shows up when there is too little sunlight and too much water.
- Crabgrass means there is too much water.
- Chicory means the soil is high in clay (low topsoil) but otherwise fertile.
- Buttercups signify wet, hard soil.
- Horse nettle favors soil high in nitrogen.
- Funitory flourishes in soils with high levels of potassium.
- Eastern bracken indicates that the soil is high in phosphorus but low in potassium.
- Redroot pigweed points to soil with high levels of nitrogen.

- Red clover identifies areas with elevated potassium levels.
- Purslane and mustard tend to indicate significant amounts of phosphorus.
- Soggy soils encourage heavy amounts of dock, horsetail, foxtails, willows, ox-eye daisy, goldenrod, poison hemlock, rushes, and sedges.
- Compacted soils are havens for plants such as chicory, knotweed, and bindweed. White lupines and sweet clover can remedy this problem; their roots are strong enough to break up the soil as they grow.
- Acidic soils foster dandelions, field peppergrass, salad burnet, scarlet pimpernel, campion, stinkweed, nodding thistle sorrel, mullein, stinging nettle, wild mustard, and wild pansy. Take advantage of this by sowing plants that thrive in this type of soil, such as hydrangeas, blueberries, rhododendrons, azaleas, endive, rhubarb, shallots, sweet potatoes, white potatoes, and watermelon. Asparagus, broccoli, beets, lettuce, onions, and spinach are also good options.
- Nutrient-deficient soil is evidenced by the growth of daisies, clover, wild carrot, mugwort, common mullein, wild parsnip, and wild radishes. Instead of fortifying the soil, consider planting produce hardy enough to thrive in poor soil conditions, such as beets, carrots, parsnips, peas, beans, legumes, radishes, sage, and thyme.

Soil pH

Healthy soil also has a good pH balance that indicates its relative acidity. Soil pH affects plant growth because it affects the availability of nutrients and the concentration of potentially plant-toxic minerals. In soils with a high pH (10 or higher), micronutrients such as iron, zinc, copper, and manganese are not readily available for plant use, which can result in the soil reaching toxic levels of magnesium and calcium. The application of materials such as those present in common fertilizers can help adjust the pH value. Knowing the general pH of the soil you are looking at will give you a clue into how much work will be needed to bring your soil to the proper level. It will also determine what type of crops you will be able to grow. Most crops prefer a range of 5.0 to 7.0 for pH but this can vary by individual plants — refer to seed or plant information to determine the needed pH level.

Wooded areas

Wooded areas are dominated by trees and will include many types of woody plants, shrubs, grasses, and mosses. Some wooded areas produce enough vegetation to permit grazing but are not usually viable for crop production. However, wild edibles such as morel mushrooms or natural decorative elements such as pinecones can be harvested from these areas. Some wooded areas on your property can provide a good windbreak and help preserve the soil. If you plant too close to a wooded area, you may find growing conditions difficult. Trees take a great deal of water and nutrients from the soil, which may affect your plants and the amount of water and nutrients they actually receive.

Edible Sulfur Shelf Mushrooms

If the property you are considering has significant amounts of wooded areas, you also can clear some of the land and sell the wood to lumber mills or firewood wholesalers. Some companies even will clear the trees free and split part of the profit with you.

Climate

Another important characteristic to consider as you set up your farm is the climate you will be working in and the plants that are hardy enough to thrive in that zone. The United States is divided into 11 hardiness zones by the USDA. Many of the colder zones have long enough growing seasons to raise most crops, however, these plants will die off during the freezing winter. This is why tropical fruit trees do not live past the mid-range zones — below zero temperatures in the winter will kill the plant. This is referred to as plant hardiness and seed packets or plant identification tags will list the appropriate zone for each plant. Methods such as hoophouses, greenhouses, and root cellars can be used to extend the growing season but these methods are often cost-prohibitive for a small farmer. It is best to choose plants suited to your zone and not try to fight Mother Nature.

USDA Hardiness Zones and Average Annual Minimum Temperature Range

Zone	Fahrenheit	Celsius	Example Cities
1	Below -50 F	Below -45.6 C	Fairbanks, Alaska; Resolute, Northwest Territories (Canada)
2a	-50 to -45 F	-42.8 to -45.5 C	Prudhoe Bay, Alaska; Flin Flon, Manitoba (Canada)
2b	-45 to -40 F	-40.0 to -42.7 C	Unalakleet, Alaska; Pinecreek, Minnesota
3a	-40 to -35 F	-37.3 to -39.9 C	International Falls, Minnesota; St. Michael, Alaska
3b	-35 to -30 F	-34.5 to -37.2 C	Tomahawk, Wisconsin; Sidney, Montana
4a	-30 to -25 F	-31.7 to -34.4 C	Minneapolis/St.Paul, Minnesota; Lewistown, Montana
4b	-25 to -20 F	-28.9 to -31.6 C	Northwood, Iowa; Nebraska
5a	-20 to -15 F	-26.2 to -28.8 C	Des Moines, Iowa; Illinois
5b	-15 to -10 F	-23.4 to -26.1 C	Columbia, Missouri; Mansfield, Pennsylvania
6a	-10 to -5 F	-20.6 to -23.3 C	St. Louis, Missouri; Lebanon, Pennsylvania
6b	-5 to 0 F	-17.8 to -20.5 C	McMinnville, Tennessee; Branson, Missouri
7a	0 to 5 F	-15.0 to -17.7 C	Oklahoma City, Oklahoma; South Boston, Virginia
7b	5 to 10 F	-12.3 to -14.9 C	Little Rock, Arkansas; Griffin, Georgia
8a	10 to 15 F	-9.5 to -12.2 C	Tifton, Georgia; Dallas, Texas
8b	15 to 20 F	-6.7 to -9.4 C	Austin, Texas; Gainesville, Florida
9a	20 to 25 F	-3.9 to -6.6 C	Houston, Texas; St. Augustine, Florida
9b	25 to 30 F	-1.2 to -3.8 C	Brownsville, Texas; Fort Pierce, Florida
10a	30 to 35 F	1.6 to -1.1 C	Naples, Florida; Victorville, California
10b	35 to 40 F	4.4 to 1.7 C	Miami, Florida; Coral Gables, Florida
11	above 40 F	above 4.5 C	Honolulu, Hawaii; Mazatlan, Mexico

Chapter 3

Type of Farm: How Do You Fit In?

T he type of farm you choose will depend on several factors such as the work you prefer doing, the resources you have available, the region you live in, and market demand for the end product. Of course, your personal interests and background will dictate how you build your business but you can incorporate some proven, profitable farm enterprises into your plan, such as selling eggs or one-season beef cows. Whichever avenue you choose, make sure it is something you will enjoy. After all, it will be your livelihood and will require your attention daily.

You also can combine many of these ventures into one farm or add one of these elements to an already existing operation. The key is to choose a venture that will meet an existing demand — you do not want to start raising chickens if your farmers' market already has two egg or broiler vendors. Also, remember that your expenses will vary by the type of farm you select — animals are much more expensive to raise than a vegetable garden. Be sure to include all potential expenses such as fuel for heat, insurance, and vet bills as you weigh the pros and cons of your farm idea.

When selecting your centerpiece agricultural activity, focus on opportunities that exhibit:

- Low startup costs relative to the potential for profit
- High profit margins after initial startup
- Relatively low maintenance costs
- High customer return rate
- High success rate among new entrepreneurs
- High product distinctiveness, since differentiation can be the key to making your products stand out
- An activity that does not have limiting economies of scale, meaning that you can start small and go big without cost becoming prohibitive

CASE STUDY: SUCCESS CAN START SMALL

Paul and Sandy Gilbertson
Armstrong Acres
Backus, MN

Armstrong Acres was founded on Sandy's grandparents' home farm in 2009. The Gilbertsons wanted to provide eggs and meat both for their own use and for sale, and so far, they have built a satisfied customer base. They raise free-range chickens and started their flock with Black Australorps and Buff Orpington layers and a few broilers. Free-range chickens are those raised without unnecessary medications or day-long confinement. The chickens are confined at night to keep them safe from predators. Predators are by far the biggest health risk to adult chickens and will steal eggs, draining profits from the farm business.

The Gilbertsons have found that the major labor requirements on their farm are cleaning the coop and record keeping. Clean housing for the chickens keeps diseases under control and ensures the eggs stay clean. Keeping good records helps them track feed intake, cost, egg production, and sales. These types of records show if the flock is producing enough eggs and meat to cover the costs of feed and other inputs. Decreased egg production may mean the layer flock is past its prime and needs to be replaced with younger, more productive hens.

Although they have only been in the business for a short time, they have found they should have done more market research in the beginning. Market demand has been exceptional, and they easily could have started out with a bigger flock. They have always and continue to sell at local farmers' markets, but this high demand has allowed them to expand their business and add a shop on the farm.

The Gilbertsons suggest that a farmer getting into the chicken-raising business start small with a flock of 25 to 30 chickens. In this manner, you can learn how to care for and market your products without making a large outlay of money. As you gain knowledge and secure steady customers, you may find that you can increase your flock size substantially into a viable farm enterprise.

Produce and Edibles

While farming may be associated with raising animals, growing produce provides a wealth of opportunities for making money or diversifying your existing product offerings. The profit margin on most garden-type produce is also quite high because these crops take little room, require minimal labor, and need only inexpensive seeds to get started. Better yet, they sell at market for a great price. Consider a typical summer weekly farmers' market: The dollar sale per customer seems low, but if 200 people spend $20 per week at your booth, you would gross $16,000 per month. If you can boost production to meet even more customers' needs, you only will increase your bottom line. On any scale, you can see selling produce at a local farmers' market has a fairly high rate of return. Furthermore, a garden does not require daily care such as when raising animals and it can give you a great foot in the door, as the startup cost is minimal.

Vegetables and herbs

There are several important considerations when farming vegetables or culinary herbs. Primarily, you will not reach the majority of consumers by selling at a farmers' market. This is because most people are largely out of touch with the growing cycles of nature and expect to find produce year-round at their grocery store. These supermarket shoppers do not care that this produce is less nutritious or not as tasty as your offerings because store-bought produce is usually less expensive. When you, as a small farmer, sell

your vegetables, these factors will affect your sales, and you will have to be somewhat of an educator and salesperson to capture new customers from the supermarket crowd. Also, it is likely that your crop will be ready for market at the same time as other farmers', so you will have lots of competition at farmers' markets.

Pay special attention to what produce is being sold by other farmers at each venue, what they charge, how they price their wares such as per piece or by the pound, and when they introduce specific varieties. Look for trends or missing items that you can use to your advantage. For example, you might find that growers run out of produce as the season wanes, maybe you could build a greenhouse to extend your growing season and provide this produce to customers at the season's end. Most people who visit farmers' markets are looking for fresh, tasty, and unique, but you also will need to compete on price and quality.

When selecting vegetables to grow you also must consider the labor and space required to bring each crop to harvest and what your return on investment will be in relation to these factors. If it takes a huge plot of land and an entire day to pick the crop, you must be able to sell your product at a profit that makes up for this labor and expense. These space and labor needs can eat into your profits, so consider carefully every input that will go into your final product.

Seasonality is also an important factor that will affect your farm's cash flow. For instance a spinach and lettuce crop will peak in the spring, but as the days heat up, you will not have much to pick. By adding crops that mature at different rates, you always will have something to bring to market. With careful planning, it is possible to have continual yields from spring to late autumn. *See Chapter 4 for more information on continual yields through succession planting.*

You also should consider general taste preferences and the amount of money people are willing to pay for particular vegetables. For example, people generally pay more for short-season crops such as asparagus or strawberries compared to more readily available crops such as sweet corn or onions. Be aware, too, that you will not be able to realize a profit unless you are able to locate a buyer.

How much do fresh vegeables cost to buy?

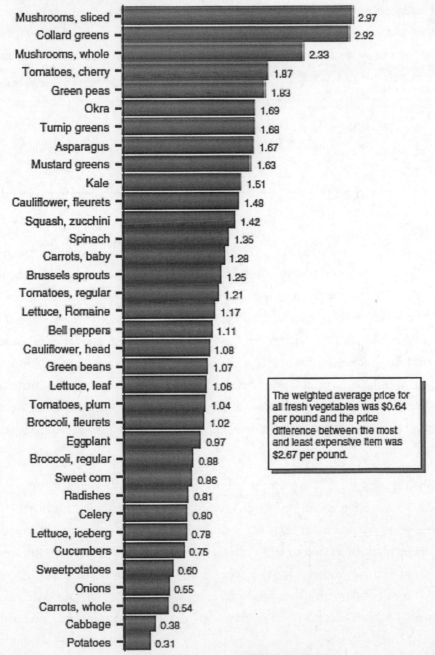

Vegetable	Dollars per pound
Mushrooms, sliced	2.97
Collard greens	2.92
Mushrooms, whole	2.33
Tomatoes, cherry	1.97
Green peas	1.83
Okra	1.69
Turnip greens	1.68
Asparagus	1.67
Mustard greens	1.63
Kale	1.51
Cauliflower, fleurets	1.49
Squash, zucchini	1.42
Spinach	1.35
Carrots, baby	1.28
Brussels sprouts	1.25
Tomatoes, regular	1.21
Lettuce, Romaine	1.17
Bell peppers	1.11
Cauliflower, head	1.08
Green beans	1.07
Lettuce, leaf	1.06
Tomatoes, plum	1.04
Broccoli, fleurets	1.02
Eggplant	0.97
Broccoli, regular	0.88
Sweet corn	0.86
Radishes	0.81
Celery	0.80
Lettuce, iceberg	0.78
Cucumbers	0.75
Sweetpotatoes	0.60
Onions	0.55
Carrots, whole	0.54
Cabbage	0.38
Potatoes	0.31

> The weighted average price for all fresh vegetables was $0.64 per pound and the price difference between the most and least expensive item was $2.67 per pound.

Dollars per pound

The produce you grow may have other uses as well. These uses are referred to as value-added opportunities because you add value by processing them into ready-to-eat foods such as sauces herb medleys, marinades, or pesto. Not only does this add product lines to your table but it also makes use of any surplus or unsold fresh produce. Additionally, you can sell your produce for non-consumer uses such as animal feed. These sales are best for produce that is not suitable for market.

 TIP! If you are selling processed or prepared foods, you may need a special food handling license or permit. Check with your local city hall for regulations.

Fruits

Fruits tend to garner higher prices than their vegetable counterparts and typically require less daily maintenance than vegetables, but it will take time to realize any profit from fruits. Trees, bushes, or vines are only planted once but will not yield produce for two or more seasons. However, once the plant is mature and the fruit is brought to bear, yields are generally high per square foot, frequently higher than many vegetables. Also, having a planting of fruit trees can serve as a windbreak, as an extra food source for animals, and as a diversification to product offerings that many consumers appreciate. Growing fruits presents many opportunities for value-added products, such as making jam or wine.

Choosing the type of fruit you would like to grow really depends on your topography and growing climate. Obviously, if you live in the northern zones, you will not be able to grow oranges. However, advances in breeding have made it easier to grow crops such as grapes in colder climates. Do some online research for the type and variety you are thinking about growing or check with other local growers in your area. Trees also will take a lot of room, so it is best if you have a good acreage to start your orchard.

Another fun way to earn money off a fruit crop is to create a "pick-your-own" experience for your customers. Perishable fruits demand a premium price but getting this fragile produce to market can be a challenge. This approach also can work for hardier seasonal produce such as apples, pumpkins, or ornamental grasses. Bringing customers directly to your farm also gives you an opportunity to showcase other offerings you may have. Just be aware that having people on your farm might create insurance issues or scare your animals; be prepared by fencing off animals well and check with your insurance agent to make sure accidents are covered.

How much does fresh fruit cost to buy?

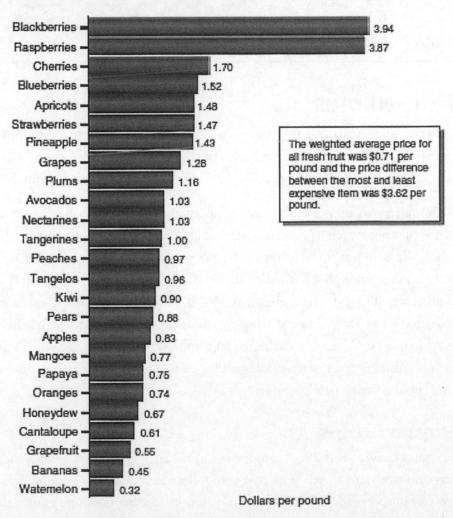

The weighted average price for all fresh fruit was $0.71 per pound and the price difference between the most and least expensive item was $3.62 per pound.

Fruit	Dollars per pound
Blackberries	3.94
Raspberries	3.87
Cherries	1.70
Blueberries	1.52
Apricots	1.48
Strawberries	1.47
Pineapple	1.43
Grapes	1.28
Plums	1.16
Avocados	1.03
Nectarines	1.03
Tangerines	1.00
Peaches	0.97
Tangelos	0.96
Kiwi	0.90
Pears	0.88
Apples	0.83
Mangoes	0.77
Papaya	0.75
Oranges	0.74
Honeydew	0.67
Cantaloupe	0.61
Grapefruit	0.55
Bananas	0.45
Watermelon	0.32

Dollars per pound

What does Heirloom mean?

These are new plants grown from the seeds of passed down through generations of plants, producing the same product year after year. Heirloom is the term typically given to seeds, and the subsequent fruit of the plants, after they have reached 50 years old. Animals, such as turkeys, also can be said to be "heirloom" or "heritage" if the result of naturally mating pairs of both grandparent and parent stock. Some consumers prefer heirloom or heritage agricultural products.

Non-edibles

Opportunities exist outside the dinner table produce aisle in non-edible items, such as flowers, perfume herbs, or dried natural items such as ornamental grasses. This practice, called floriculture, is a $10-billion industry.

Although growing non-edibles as a primary crop is uncommon for a small farm, plantings such as flowers and aromatic herbs have quite a market in wholesale bath and toiletry products. While the average small farmer will not produce enough to sell directly to large companies, you can find a market by selling to wholesalers. You also can find buyers in local specialty markets where people are looking for the raw ingredients to make their own soaps, perfume, or candles. In fact, look down the row at your next farmers' market, and you probably will see someone selling these items — this could be your new customer.

Hay and straw

Hay and straw are another example of a non-edible farming product. Both hay and straw are planted as a cover crop, then harvested and sold for a variety of purposes. While this practice is common, other cover crops may be more beneficial, be it because of the integrity of the soil or inherent profits. The cost of harvesting the hay or straw also must be considered; many other cover crops do not require harvesting but are simply tilled directly into the soil.

Animal Byproducts

Keeping your own chickens and milking your own cows are activities that invoke the quintessential image of farming. Animal byproducts, such as eggs or milk, are popular items for small farmers and can be very profitable. Even keeping just a few chickens can provide a few dozen eggs per week. Even if animal byproducts only provide enough for your own family's use, the cost of the animals themselves can be offset by the work they can contribute to the farm, such as the way that chickens often till the ground pecking for food, or the way cows keep grass short and provide fertilizer. Be sure to check with your local government for regulations particular to keeping animals on your land

Chickens for meat or for eggs

A broiler chicken is a chicken raised specifically for consumption, rather than its eggs or siring chicks. The market for chicken meat is huge with a per capita consumption higher than beef and trending up. The demand for free-range or organic chickens is even higher as factory-farmed poultry continues to get bad press. In addition, farm fresh eggs are a sought after commodity both by private consumers and high-end restaurants. Be sure to check with your local government to determine any restrictions are regarding the size and location of your coop. Many cities now allow two or three chickens in a backyard coop but no roosters.

Having chickens on your farm is also beneficial to your land and actually can improve your garden. By using temporary fencing or pens, you can move the chickens around and as they peck for roots they aerate the ground, their waste is great fertilizer, and they will eat pests off your plants. Furthermore, chickens can be raised on just about any type of land, including the unused edges of a field. The quick turnaround of eight weeks from chick to broiler also makes raising broilers a good moneymaker.

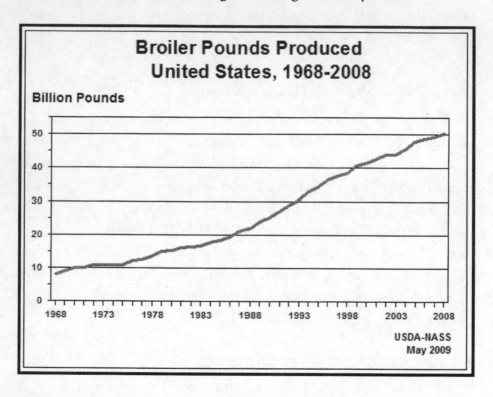

Dairy cows

Dairy farming can help you diversify your product line and provide the opportunity for value-added products such as butter or cheese. Even if you do not know how to make cheese or butter, this is something you could outsource or develop through partnerships with another company or local artisan. Of course, a dairy operation is labor-intensive, heavily regulated, and requires a lot of specialized equipment. With the right background and setup, though, you can see a good profit through dairy cows.

If you have knowledge of pasture quality and fertility management, raising grass-based dairy cows can offer a good return on investment because you eliminate the high cost of feed. One Jersey cow produces, on average, 800 gallons of milk annually. At current market prices of approximately $3.50 per gallon, you would gross $2,800 a year per cow. Cash flow for seasonally milked dairy cows will typically only occur for eight to nine months of the year.

If you would like to keep a dairy farm, a sizable portion of land should be allocated for that purpose. In fact, cows that live most of their life confined to a barn or lot around the barn have significantly shorter life spans than dairy cattle allowed access to pasture. A good dairy cow, if kept with free pasture, can have a productive life of ten years or longer. You also will need buildings to house the animals and to set up a milking parlor.

CASE STUDY: FROM CALF TO COW

Duane Spielman
Carmen Odegaard
Evansville, MN

Duane Spielman and Carmen Odegaard raise young dairy cattle as a side income on their small farm in Evansville, Minnesota. Spielman works at a large dairy that milks around 300 to 400 cows while Odegaard works as a veterinarian at local veterinary clinics. They purchase the calves from Spielman's employer and raise them from newborns to feeder calf size — around 400 to 500 pounds.

The calves are brought to their farm when they are 1 to 2 days old. Spielman makes certain the calves get at least one gallon of colostrum within the first 24 hours of life. Colostrum is a type of milk that mammals produce specifically for newborns. This is the most important factor in having a healthy calf, as after 24 hours the calf is unable to absorb the colostrum, which it uses to build its immune system. Another important factor in raising healthy calves is keeping anything the calf might touch with its mouth very clean. This includes bottles, nipples, pails, and pens.

They prefer to keep their calves in calf huts made of molded plastic. These huts are easy to move and can be bleached between calves. Each calf has its own hut which cuts down on disease transmission. When the calves are weaned, they are moved into a group pen of eight to ten calves with access to the outside. Dry air, light, and dry straw are a must in the pens.

They do not recommend purchasing baby calves from a sales barn; rather try to find a local producer and buy calves directly from the farm. You can never know for sure if a calf from the sales barn received its colostrum. Also, comingling of calves at sales barns is a probable way to transmit diseases. Spielman and Odegaard also recommend talking with a local veterinarian to find out what reputable farms will sell dairy calves. Plus, it is good to establish a working relationship with a veterinarian clinic in case medical advice or treatment is needed at any point.

The most time-consuming period when raising dairy calves is the first week when calves have to be trained to drink. The calves are fed three quarts of milk twice a day, more if the weather is very cold. They will place homemade calf jackets on the calves as well to help them retain body heat. Their health will be closely monitored as scours or diarrhea is a big killer of young calves. Any calf that appears ill gets prompt, aggressive medical treatment. The calves will be weaned by 4 to 6 weeks of age; after this the daily time commitment decreases greatly.

Spielman's best advice is to not go into debt when starting out farming. The cattle market is a tricky beast. By keeping out of debt and carefully monitoring feed costs, you can realize a profit from your calf farm enterprise.

Goats (milk and other dairy)

Keeping goats is a good option for the would-be dairy farmer. In fact, in the specialty cheese market, 96 percent buy goat cheese as well as cow's milk cheese. Raw goat's milk also typically garners more per pound than its cow-milk counterpart, and goat's milk cheese can go from $13 to $24 per pound, compared to the $4 to $6 garnered by an average cow's milk cheese.

It takes seven to nine goats to produce as much milk as one cow does. However, goats are cheaper investments and require less food and maintenance than dairy cows. Goats are also great grazers and will help keep your grass short.

Sheep (wool)

While sheep may be bred for meat or dairy, wool is becoming an increasingly popular reason to breed sheep. Wool goes for anywhere from $1 to $15 per pound. While wool garners its highest prices when used to spin yarn for consumer use, it has many non-apparel uses including hand-woven rugs, wall coverings, quilting applications, and pressed felts. In 2008, 4.7 million sheep were shorn in the U.S., producing 34.2 million pounds of wool, or 7.3 pounds per sheep. Texas and California are the most popular states for sheep production, boasting 830,000 head of sheep and 610,000 head of sheep respectively.

Animals for Food

Raising large animals such as cattle or pigs for food takes approximately ten times the energy and resources required to raise plants. Your initial investment is high as you will need to build your herd, buy all the necessary feed and equipment, and provide shelter for them. Animals also require care throughout the day, every single day — taking a vacation day means hiring someone to do your chores and check on your animals. You will incur potentially large vet bills and can expect some loss due to a number of causes, including predators, health problems, theft, poisoning, accidents, and birthing. These inputs mean a much slimmer profit margin for the small farmer, making it hard to compete with large animal operations. Whether you choose to raise animals for food is a personal choice, one that requires careful consideration of the resources you can allot and your own goals.

In fairness, meat consumption is expected to double within the next 40 years; so the market is certainly there. Americans eat an average of 8 ounces of meat per day and the specialty market for organically raised or grass-fed animals is growing. Many consumers also have moved away from super-market meat and are willing to buy meat directly from the producer — usually at a much higher per pound price. You will need to put some extra effort into marketing, though, to find and maintain and good customer base. If your product is consistently high quality you can expect word-of-mouth to build your brand. A great entry into the beef market is to raise seasonal beef. This method requires you to care for the cattle for only one season: you buy heavy calves of 500 pounds or more in the spring, let them pasture graze all summer, and sell them for beef in the fall. This gives you a better return on investment because the only equipment you need is electric fencing and a trailer to get them to market. Furthermore, you will not need to house them or feed them over the cold winter months.

Breeding animals or raising livestock for food production is not something to take on as a large-scale interest unless you have some knowledge of everything involved. If you do not have any practical experience, consider working on that type of farm for a season, or finding a farmer that is willing to mentor you. If you are unable to find a paid position, consider volunteering your services. The time investment will be well worth it in the end as you will gain valuable insight into the industry and the practical matters involved. You also will make good industry connections that will be helpful in bringing your product to market.

Chapter 4

Starting Plant Production: Where Do You Begin?

ow that you have explored your possibilities and refined your idea, it is time to get down to business. You have determined the type of farm and product you want, assessed your skills and resources, and now you need to research the production process required to develop your product. Visit similar producers or do some research at your local library to learn more about best practices for your farm. Research what elements contribute to good production and what the key factors are in producing good quality and high yields. Review the technology and latest advancements as they relate to your operation. Many of these answers are covered in industry-specific magazines or discussed at local trade group meetings in your area. Even a simple sit-down at your café to talk shop can gain you valuable industry knowledge. Now is also good time to meet with your local extension agent and

learn about government programs as they apply to your plan. Chapter 10 will talk in detail about the wide range of programs available to you. These valuable resources should be at the top of your list as you make your plan.

This chapter will cover the issues as they relate to produce, herbs, and flowers production while the following chapter will talk about raising animals. Some issues such as budget or buildings apply to both plants and animals, so those topics will be covered in this chapter.

Developing an Action Plan

The first thing you need is an action plan. It could be as simple as something drawn on the back of an envelope, but your action plan will be an important tool as you go along. Your action plan should outline the layout of your farm buildings, the placement of crops for this year and beyond, timetables for sowing seeds, maintenance and harvest schedules, and long-term planning for preserving your soil's integrity or expanding your growing spaces. You also need a plan for how, when, and where you will sell your product. Remember to include important tax and legal dates on your plan, such as when to apply for crop assistance.

Your action plan is based as much on your own preferences as on established practices and there is no right way to create your plan. Look at your operation as a business and develop a plan that makes sense to you. This plan, too, will change with time, and as you gain more experience in the field, you can adjust your plan accordingly. Every action plan, though, needs a few elements critical to a successful farm.

Budget

Creating and following a budget is the most important thing you can do to make sure you are maximizing your money. Remember to factor in all of the costs associated with your farm, including the cost of labor, seed or feed, fuel, fertilizer, marketing fees, taxes and permits, and equipment maintenance. Add incidentals such as work clothes, Internet fees, meals while you are in the field, and even sunscreen or bottled water. Try to build in an emergency fund, too, to cover any expenses related to storm damage or crop loss.

In addition to a yearly budget, every two years or so, expect to make a large capital improvement outlay, such as buying a new tractor, shed, or building renovation. Allot another $10,000 per year or so to cover these expenses. Furthermore, budget in a salary for yourself and mortgage or loan payments you have attached to the farm.

A well-thought-out budget will help you assess objectively how much money you need to start your farm and keep it running. You will see from the beginning if your farm can be profitable. Every year as you rewrite your budget, it also will help you find ways to save money by identifying expenses that could be trimmed or opportunities for expanding your markets.

Buildings

Aside from your house, you likely will want a garage or shed to keep your equipment out of the elements, storage areas for fertilizers and tools, and coops, pens, or barns for animals. For produce, you will need a place to store vegetables safely until you can get them to market and possibly a cold-storage cellar for root vegetables. This storage can be simple as long as the produce stays fresh and is protected from critters. Depending on the size of your harvest, this could be as small as an extra refrigerator or as large as a full-sized, climate-controlled steel shed. To avoid storage needs and to keep the produce at its highest quality, pick your crops as close to delivery day as possible. If you are planning to process or cook your produce, you also will need a food-safety-certified kitchen and space to store the finished product.

Produce selection, spacing, and arrangement

When planning the location of the various elements of your farm, take care in arranging your crop placement so plants receive optimal growing conditions. Each fruit, vegetable, herb, or flower prefers different topsoil depth, spacing, water, and sunlight. Some plants do not grow well next to each other, while others make great companions. For example, you can extend your leafy greens' growing season if you plant them next to taller plants that will provide shade during the heat of the day. Make sure you also allow room to move between rows or sections of plantings to make harvesting easier. Most gardening books will highlight these planting issues, or you can find helpful information online by searching according to your zone and plant selection.

Selecting a variety of produce that matures at varying times also will extend your season and your product offerings. For example, from one garden you can harvest a spring crop of spinach, an early summer collection of peas, summertime beans or tomatoes, and autumn squashes and leafy greens. With this wide variety, you always will have something  to bring to market. You also can put in the same crop such as beans or cucumbers but stagger your planting over a few weeks. Just make sure your final planting has enough time to mature and that these plants will withstand the hot, dry days of late summer. This practice is called succession planting and is actually more suitable for a small farm without large acres of one type of crop. Not only will successive planting reduce stress caused by having everything come to bear at once, it also will ensure that you have continual offerings for your selling venue.

With a well-planned successive planting schedule, even a small plot of land can yield between 30 and 40 varieties throughout the growing season. If you decide to start a midsummer crop, expect the flavors to be a bit milder. Also, many seeds go dormant when the temperature gets above 80 degrees Fahrenheit. You can start seeds inside in these conditions but after planting outside, the new seedlings will have to be protected from the heat. To be sure of a harvest, plant seeds so you will have at least eight weeks before a typical frost. Some good mid-season plantings include:

- Leafy greens such as arugula, spinach, or Swiss chard
- Herbs such as dill, basil, cilantro, or parsley
- Root crops such as beets, turnips, or rutabagas
- Vining crops such as green beans or snap peas

Cyclic farming is also a great way to try out different crops each year. Without a large investment of time or money, you can add a few plants here and there to see how they do at market. If they do well, next year you can expand those plantings. At the least, it will add extra interest to your sales booth.

HOW TO: Map Out Your Plantings.

To plan out your plantings, use the same method decorators use to design a room to scale. Using grid paper, create an easy-to-read key, such as one square equals one foot. Start by drawing the perimeter of your planting space, making sure to mark locations of fences, water spigots, topography, and potential shade issues. Once you have the base area marked, make copies so you can plan your successive plantings — you will need a page for spring, summer, and fall plantings (if you live in a temperate zone.) Review the spacing requirements needed for each plant and place on your layout, making sure to leave room for pathways.

Your garden can grow vertically, too, and by growing it upward, you will nearly double its space. Many plants, such as cucumbers, beans, squashes, and peas, can be trained to grow up a trellis or teepee-style structure, and they actually will grow better because they will not be competing with weeds or touching the soil. Be sure to position trellises — and taller plants such as corn or tomatoes — on the northern or eastern edges of your garden where they will still get plenty of sun without shading the rest of your garden unless you need them to shade leafy greens. Save your garden plan as a handy reference for next year's crop rotation.

As mentioned earlier, your produce also might allow you to expand your product line by processing your yield into jams, sauces, or marinades. These products add variety to your overall product offerings and can expand your sales volume but also require more labor and supplies. Before jumping into a value-added product offering, first consider:

- What are the projected costs and returns for getting involved with this product?
- If things do not go well, can I use the equipment or try something else?
- Would it be better to work with a coprocessor to test the market first?
- Am I using byproducts in this scenario or would I be using products that would sell just as well on their own?
- What regulations relate to this product?
- Do I need special licenses or inspections to process these items and sell them?

Tomato Sauce

CASE STUDY: A FARM OF BIBLICAL PROPORTIONS

Bartlett Farm
1854 107th St NE
Bottineau, ND 58318
office@bartlettfarm.us
www.bartlettfarm.us
701-263-4574

The Bartlett family has a diversified, direct-marketing farm. They raise many different products: beef, pork, chickens, turkeys, fruits, and vegetables. Their overriding farm goal is to provide clean, healthy, and natural food to local customers in accordance with biblical guidelines for life.

The diversity of products helps the Bartletts maximize the potential of their land and provide job security to the family because their income is derived from multiple venues and not tied to market fluctuations.

Additionally, they feel they can better serve their customer base by offering a wide variety of products as different products attract different people.

They started out by selling vegetables at a local farmers' market. By the next summer, they found a ready-made market for their raspberry crop at the nearby convenience store located near Lake Metigoshe, a recreational area with many summer lake cabins. They passed out brochures and business cards everywhere they went and soon the market found them. Rather than researching a market, they simply began by advertising the family's surplus products.

The Bartletts lived in a city for many years before becoming farmers and did not even plan to start farming for a living. It grew out of providing for their own food needs. As their family grew, they realized the importance of becoming entrepreneurs to achieve their dreams of self-sufficiency, keeping the family together, and instilling a Christian work ethic. The best aspect of farming for them was the ability to involve the entire family in the business. Instead of everyone going their separate ways, each person was given a unique responsibility that contributed to the overall well-being of the farm. The lifestyle that farming brought has been ideal for teaching children character and a diligent Christian work ethic.

The Bartletts advise others desiring to enter the farming life to not cut corners. They learned this the hard way when their chickens did not thrive due to their diet of straight flax screenings. Now they buy the mineral supplements their animals need, even though it is expensive. They also feel that sometimes you need to forge ahead and start doing something even if you don't feel like you know enough to begin. You will learn along the way, and find out what questions need to be asked. If necessary, start with a few mixed-breed animals, and upgrade after you have learned how to take care of them properly. Do not be afraid to step into the unknown.

In addition, they suggest that the beginning farmer remain debt free. Even though beginning a small farm is difficult, finances should increase parallel with the learning curve. Debt will enslave you to the bank and cause you to make choices that you may regret in hindsight. Starting with a smaller amount of costs is the surest way to guide your purchases in the wisest direction, keep your farm independent and stable, and help ensure long-term prosperity.

The Bartletts are optimistic about the future market for their products and see continued need for alternatives as the American population becomes more aware of the detrimental effects of conventional chemical farming and processed foods. They feel they are positioned well for this shift as more and more people look for their food through, local diversified farms.

Getting Into the Action

Once you have a good plan and everything lined up, it is time to get to work. Bringing your produce to market begins with the seed and ends with taking care of your soil until next year's planting. It is an ongoing cycle and as a farmer, you always will have a reason to be working the land. As the seasons progress from planning to harvesting, you will learn to live more in tune with the lifecycle of your farm. There really is no start and endpoint — to get you going, though, we will start your work list with late winter and early spring.

Most of your chores will be plant- or farm-specific such as when and where to plant or how to harvest and store each variety. Visit your local library or bookstore and stock up on books related to the type of produce you will grow. Consider subscribing to trade magazines or general farming magazines such as *Mother Earth News* or *Grit*. These publications will give you specific instructions and keep you current on industry trends.

Selecting seeds or plants

Once you have decided on what vegetables or fruits you want to grow, the next step is buying your seeds, starting seedlings, or buying plants from a nursery. You can find just about any variety of seed or plant plus gardening

supplies through online gardening websites or large seed companies such as Gurney's® or Burpee®. You can also buy heirloom varieties through Seed Savers® or Rare Seeds websites or through local gardener's clubs. As a small farmer — especially if you are selling at farmers' markets — look for unique varieties that others might not grow. Whatever you choose to grow, be sure to order your seeds early, and choose plants suited to your growing conditions. When purchasing seeds, you may be able to save some money by buying them in bulk. However, seeds have a certain life expectancy, so be sure not to buy more than you can use each year. It is possible to store seeds until next season, but they must be protected from temperature extremes and moisture. Considering the relatively low cost of seeds, it is better to buy new every year so you are assured of a good crop.

Many people start seeds indoors and then transplant them into the garden once they have developed into strong seedlings. This method allows you to control your own growing conditions, avoid nursery-bred diseases or pests, and get a jump-start on the growing season. Starting your own seeds does require extra equipment and a heated space while the seeds are sprouting. You will need grow lights, containers, or flats for planting the seeds, a watering system or spray bottles, tables to hold everything, and time to care for your seedlings. Many plants do not need to be started early and can be planted directly in the garden as soon as the soil is warm enough and the threat of frost has passed. Refer to your gardening books or seed catalogs for seed starting instructions and planting recommendations for each plant.

If you are fond of a particular variety of vegetable or flower, consider saving the seeds. Remember that most hybrid varieties will not produce viable seeds, so be careful to select seeds from heirloom or non-hybrid plants. Some plants, too, such as hollyhock or cabbage are biennials and will not produce seeds until their second season. Refer to your favorite gardening book or website for information on harvesting seeds from your specific plant. Once the seeds are harvested and completely dried, label them, and store them separately in airtight containers. Avoid exposure to light while in storage.

Preparing the soil and planting your crops

As a new farmer, you might have some work cut out for you as you get your planting areas ready. If the land you are planting is wooded, pastureland, or has stood unused for some time, you will need to clear the land and till the soil. Trees can be cleared at any time, but you will have wait for the soil to thaw before tilling. On new land, you must break up big chunks of soil, eliminate large rocks or roots, and create a smooth bed in which you can plant. The best tool for this is a large rototiller or tractor with tiller attachment — it will be a back-breaking chore and can take some time if you are doing it manually. Once the initial tilling is done, though, it will take less work each season to keep the land in good shape. Most seasons you can till the ground with a small rototiller or a sturdy shovel. You also might need to make amendments or additions to your soil to keep it at maximum fertility. Tips on maintaining your soil will be covered later in this chapter.

Once you have the soil in tip-top shape, you can start planting. Refer to the seed packet or plant packaging for specifics on planting depth, spacing, and expected time to harvest. If you are using successive planting, follow the plan you have devised. If you are putting in seedlings or plants, make sure the night temperatures stay above freezing or be prepared to cover up your plants on these nights. Seeds, new plants, and bulbs are also a tasty treat for squirrels and other critters, so clean up any debris left over from planting. You will be fighting marauders throughout the growing season, so consider putting in a fence or row coverings to protect your crops.

Growing season chores

As the seedlings emerge and your garden begins to fill in, your chores now are focused on keeping conditions right for optimal growth. You must eliminate the weeds, or they will rob your plants of nutrients and water. Weeding with a hoe or tractor attachment can be effectively as long as the blades do not damage the roots of the existing plants. Hand-weeding around delicate new plants is the safest method until they are established. Once the plant is able to grow full and bushy, the weeds will not be able to take hold. Mulching between rows and around plants is also a good way to control weed growth.

Keeping plants well watered is also important. Not only does inadequate water affect the plants' growth, but it also can alter the taste and quality of the produce. Water requirements vary greatly by species, by region, and by type of soil so educate yourself on these needs as you choose your plants. Selecting plants suited to your growing environment will make it easier to meet water demands. Just make sure you have a way to access water for all your crops for times of drought. Mulching is also a great way to retain water in your soil.

As your plants mature, you will need to prune them or train them to grow up a trellis. This can be done every few days as you check over your plants or pick things have ripened. Pick off dead leaves or misshapen produce and look for signs of disease — some diseases can spread quickly so it is best to remove the plant entirely. Do not put diseased plant debris in a compost pile as the spores can linger in this soil and spread to a new garden. Look for bugs, too, and remove as many as possible. Most people who buy from farmers' markets want pesticide-free produce, so look for organic ways to fight pests. Consider getting a couple of chickens and keeping them in your garden, as they are great bug eaters.

While you work in your gardens, keep mental notes of how things are going. Do you see an area that has poor drainage or gets too much shade? You can fix these issues in the off-season or mark as areas to avoid planting next year. Even in the midst of this growing season, you should be considering your future plans.

Harvesting

It can be difficult to know when to harvest your produce because you are picking items for market, not for your own consumption. For home use, you would pick the day you plan on eating it or processing it, usually

Harvesting potatoes

at its ripest state. For market, though, you must plan on bringing produce your customers can keep for a couple days before eating — for this reason, you will need to pick produce that is just ripe enough to be attractive, yet not too ripe, so it can survive for several days after purchase. You also may find that harvesting some items early gives the plants more time to produce additional yields.

Each variety has different harvest clues but here a few pointers for choosing when to harvest some common fruits and vegetables:

- **Cucumbers:** While the optimum length and girth of a cucumber depends on the particular variety, all cucumbers should be picked when their seeds are half their full size. Furthermore, most varieties should be dropped into cold water after harvesting in order to maintain crispness.

- **Eggplants:** The best way to tell if an eggplant is ready to be picked is to press it lightly with your thumb. If it springs back quickly, it is ready to be picked; if it cannot be indented, it is too soon; and if the dent remains, you have waited too long. Larger eggplants tend to be bitter.

- **Broccoli:** Many people tend to harvest the central head of the broccoli plant when it comes to maturity in an effort to stimulate the growth of the offshoots. Instead, when the broccoli plant has grown three leaves and the center head has just begun to develop, twist the center head off. The broccoli then will form larger side shoots.

- **Corn:** Corn is ready to be picked when the kernels are tender and juicy and when a milky white liquid oozes out after a kernel is pierced. The silk of the stalks also should be dry.

- **Watermelon:** Knocking watermelons to know when they are ripe is a tried-and-true test; immature melons sound metallic, while ripe melons produce a dull thud. Another, somewhat easier, way to discern ripeness is if the tendril where the fruit stem meets the vine has died; this means the watermelon is ripe.

- **Tomatoes:** While tomatoes usually are left for picking until they are just nearly ripe, consider picking a few when they are still green. There is quite a market for green tomatoes; many consumers enjoy them fried or pickled that way, and it is a good way to establish a "tomato relationship" with a consumer before a competitor can.

Post-Harvest Work

Once the fields are cleared and the end-of-the-season is upon you, you will need to do a few chores to prepare your fields for next year. Start by clearing as much plant debris as possible to remove potential diseased plants. Do not just throw it all away, though, as many people love natural elements such as cornstalks for home decorating. Healthy plant debris is also a great addition to your compost pile. Many farmers choose to till their land after harvest, but in most cases, this is not necessary, as leaving some roots or groundcover will protect your soil from erosion over the winter. This is also a good time of year to repair broken tools and make sure everything is stored away for the winter. Many garden supply stores also put merchandise on clearance, so look through these aisles for supplies you might need next season.

Soil maintenance

After a strenuous growing season, your land might be in need of some extra attention. As plants grow, they remove nutrients from the soil, and over time, this can deplete the soils' fertility significantly. This depletion can be repaired by tilling in good quality compost or well-aged manure. This task also can be done in the spring, but it is usually easier to do in the autumn because the ground will not be soggy or mushy from spring thaws. Additionally, amendments put in during the fall have more time to break down before planting time.

A compost pile is not difficult to maintain but can be smelly, messy, and attract critters. Some folks opt for a turning barrel-type compost system that is essentially a closed container with some holes for air flow. These are not typically big enough to produce enough compost for a small farm. If you have room on your property for a compost pile, be sure to locate it well away from your living area, and be prepared to work it around every few days.

A simpler method to fortifying soil without dealing with a compost pile is to add kitchen waste directly to the garden during the growing season. These items can be buried with the plants or trenched in alongside the rows of vegetable. Be aware, though, that large chunks of food will take a long time to breakdown and might attract critters looking for a free meal. These include:

- Coffee grounds
- Used tea leaves
- Cut up banana peels
- Carrot or potato peelings
- Potato peelings
- Cooking water (i.e. pasta, steaming vegetables)
- Eggshells
- Leafy tops of vegetables

If you found that your produce did not yield well and soil amendments did not work, you may want to check the pH of your soils. Kits are available at your local extension office, and they can help you determine the right type and amount of concentrates to apply, such as adding phosphorous to combat a low pH level.

Crop rotation

One way to protect the quality of your soil from year to year is to rotate the location of each crop. Different plants take different nutrients from the soil, and vegetables within the same family take similar nutrients from the soil. Over time, the soil can become depleted nutritionally if the same family crop is planted repeatedly in the same location.

Vegetable families

Chenopodiaceae	Beet Chard Spinach
Solanaceae	Potato Tomato Peppers
Cucurbitaceae	Cucumber Melon Squash
Aliaceae	Garlic Leek Onion Shallot
Leguminoseae (Fabaceae)	Alfalfa Beans Peas Clover Vetch Lentils
Umbelliferae	Carrot Celeriac Celery Fennel Parsley Parsnip Dill
Compositae (Asteraceae)	Endive Jerusalem artichoke Lettuce Salsify

Brassicaceae (Cruciferae)	Broccoli Cabbage Cauliflower Kale Radish Turnip Brussels sprouts Oriental brassicas Mustard Kohlrabi
Miscellaneous	Corn New Zealand spinach Rye Buckwheat Mache

By alternating or rotation crop locations each year, the soil will have time to replenish itself, and you will have higher yields and healthier plants. Refer to your yearly garden plan as you decide placement of next year's crops. Most crops can be rotated on a two-year basis — check by variety in your gardening books or search online for "crop rotation planning."

Soil erosion

Wind, water, and even animal traffic can be quite a destructive force on your land, especially when it is bare between seasons. Rainfall or melting snow breaks down soil aggregates, washes away fertile topsoil, and leaves behind compacted, dense soil that is not conducive to healthy plant growth. Naturally, land with a steeper slope will experience greater soil loss from erosion by water. If your land has long slopes, plant your fields across the slope using narrow swatches — often referred to as contour planting. This will protect your planted fields by slowing surface runoff as it moves down the incline. Vegetation and residue combinations, such as alfalfa or winter crop stubble also will offer some protection during the winter.

Soil erosion by wind works the same way as erosion by water — lighter and finer particles are transported more easily than heavier particles. Windbreaks such as trees, shrubs, or cover crops will slow down the wind's force and help anchor your soils to the surface. Large, unplanted fields or exposed knolls are most vulnerable to the wind's power and benefit greatly from cover crops or crop residue.

It is quite easy to determine if your fields are being eroded. After a rainstorm you will see long grooves throughout your field — and often a muddy patch at the bottom of the groove. This muddy patch is topsoil that has been moved by the water. If you see dust clouds on windy days or behind your tractor as you till, this is wind erosion relocating your fertile land. Erosion on some scale will take place no matter what you do but there are ways to combat erosion and protect your topsoil. Stop by your local farm bureau or extension office for help in dealing with the erosion on your farm. They can offer assistance in planting cover crops, putting in windbreaks, or developing contour planting plans. Working on erosion control solutions is easier to accomplish during the off-season because you have a lighter farm workload and do not have growing crops to work around.

Grape vineyard planted using contour planting.

Chapter 5

Beginning
Animal Production

A nimal production ranges from the simple to the complex and compared to raising produce, requires more advanced skills, special accommodations, and expensive equipment. The costly inputs needed such as feed, shelter and health care can make for slim profit margins. Poultry or other small animals such as rabbits are probably the easiest livestock species to raise on a small-scale farm. They require minimal space and housing, are easy to care for, and actually can be beneficial to your farm through grazing or eating bugs. Beef cattle, sheep or goats for meat or wool, and pigs require a bit more care but often only need a sturdy fence and a standard barn. These animals also need little human care beyond basic feeding and water — and might not even need that if they are allowed enough room to roam.

The most complex animal operation is a dairy farm, be it cows or goats. Dairy cattle need to be milked twice a day and must have a clean, warm barn to live in with access to sufficient grazing. Milking or cheese making requires specialized equipment, and the raw product is subject to stringent FDA rules and regulations. Furthermore, you have lots of competition for the end-product from large dairy farms.

If you are new to farming with animals, you must educate yourself thoroughly before filling your coops or pastures. The initial outlay for animals, equipment, feed, and housing is quite expensive, and if you do not know what you are doing, the animals will not thrive. This chapter will give you a good starting point on each animal. Research your choice further by checking your local library, doing an online search, or by visiting with a local farmer. If you grew up farming but do not have the funds to start your own full operation, you can co-op with another farmer to share space and equipment to house your own livestock. Many times, these arrangements require you to split your profits or provide labor for the farmer, but it is a great way to get started.

Many of the business-related activities mentioned in the previous chapter — including budgeting, planning, marketing, and good land-management practices — also apply to livestock farming. Review those sections if you have not already read through them. Many small farmers find ways to combine livestock production with a produce-raising venture. The two fit together well, as you can feed your leftover produce to the animals, and the animals can help control weeds and bugs and give you back nutrient-rich fertilizer. Your selling venues, too, will overlap, and you often can sell a "basket" of all your goods to one customer. Just make sure you have the time, energy, and resources to support each venture fully and consistently produce a high-quality product.

Chickens

Chickens are arguably the most farm-friendly livestock to raise. The start-up costs and overall expenses of a small flock of chickens are the lowest of all livestock species. They offer the quickest to turnaround from birth to market. Whether you have a trio of hens to provide your family with fresh eggs or a barn full of broilers for meat, raising chickens is a fun, profitable, first step to starting your farming journey.

Chickens can be raised in almost any building, provided it is draft-free and predator proof. As the chicks grow, they will need space for nesting, feeding, and watering. The mini-mum amount of space for a broiler of lightweight layer is one square foot. Heavier or larger birds will require twice that amount. More floor space and room to roam keeps diseases from spreading through your flock. Brand new chicks still in the down stage are un-

Secured pen for hens.

able to regulate body heat, so they need a constant source of external heat and protection from wind. Their immune systems are also less capable of fighting off disease, so extra attention should be paid to keeping their environment clean and reasonably sanitary. They also need a constant source of fresh water and chick starter feed.

Purchase your chicks from a reputable source whose top priority is hatching healthy chicks. Mail-order companies or feedstore purchases are fine, provided they can tell you the source of their chicks. Make sure the chicks were hatched in a reputable hatchery not in a backyard with question-able sanitation standards. Chickens come in different breeds: laying breeds, meat breeds, and dual-purpose breeds and can be combined in your barn-yard as long as you have sufficient room.

When purchasing chicks, you can select between cockerels (males), pullets (females), or a straight-run (mix of both sexes.) If you plan on butchering your chickens for meat, cockerels are the best choice as males will put on more meat than females. If your plans include a laying flock, you obviously will need pullets. You do not need a rooster in order to get eggs. A straight–run group generally will cost a little less per chick then a group segregated by sex. Most hatcheries guarantee you will get around a 95-percent sexed group — meaning the chicken sexer has determined the accurate sex of 95 chicks out of 100, so do not be too surprised if one of your pullets is actu-ally a rooster when it matures.

At around four to five weeks of age, your chicks will be fully feathered out and large enough to move out of their brooding pen. The requirements for

a chicken coop remain the same as one for chicks: safe and secure from predators, dry, and protected from heavy winds. A shed or an unused part of a building can be used to keep the chickens. Keep them confined to their new home for a few days, then, let

them outside to scratch and peck during the daylight hours. They will come home to roost when evening approaches, where they should be locked in for the night.

Even free-range chickens might need a little extra feed so be sure to provide proper nutrition and clean water at all times. Depending on the type of bird, your chickens also might need special supplements and minerals. Ask your local vet for more information.

Ducks and Geese

Ducks and geese offer many benefits to the small-scale farmer by providing meat, weed control, and, in the case of geese, even a natural alarm system. After the first few weeks of life, ducks and geese are fairly easy to keep  and make great foragers for bugs and weeds. Ducklings or goslings also can be purchased directly from the hatchery or through feed stores. They will come in a straight-run (both sexes) or they can be sexed if you want to have more females or males. Generally a straight-run will be a few cents cheaper to purchase than those segregated by sex and is adequate when raising them for meat. If you want to breed ducks, you may want them sexed so you can have a proper ratio of males to females. One drake (male duck) will breed with five to six females. Most ganders (male geese) will only breed with one or two females.

A plot of pasture enclosed by a 3-foot, woven-wire fence makes a great feed source for both ducks and geese when they are about six weeks old. They are great at foraging for both bugs and plants. An acre of pasture can support up to 40 ducks or 20 geese. An overcrowded pasture will quickly become defoliated and heavily soiled. Ducks and geese do not care for alfalfa or tough, narrow-leaved grasses, but prefer brome grass, timothy grass, orchard grass, bluegrass, and clover. Clean, fresh water always should be available along with a place for the geese and ducks to bathe.

 TIP! Poultry feathers, especially the valuable hackles, are a high-priced commodity in the craft and fishing tackle market. Check online for wholesalers looking to build their inventory or visit your local retailers for selling opportunities.

Turkeys

Much like chickens and waterfowl, young turkeys need shelter, an external heat source, and plenty of food and starter feed when they are young. At maturity, turkeys need 20 square feet each for housing. Part of this housing could consist of an outside run — a fenced-in area that allows the birds to have access to fresh air and sunlight. Even if you provide an outdoor run for your birds, the building you use for turkey growing will need to be well ventilated. This can be as simple as having a few windows that can be propped open or as complex as an exhaust fan installed in the wall. Ammonia fumes from manure build up if the bedding is not cleaned frequently and can lead to death losses due to respiratory distress and infection.

Turkeys also do well when given access to pasture. When planning your turkey pasturing operation, expect to stock 50 young birds per acre. The best forages to plant for a turkey pasture are legumes like alfalfa or clovers and grasses like timothy grass, orchard grass, or rye grass. Although forage will be a part of their diet, they still will need to obtain a substantial amount of their food intake from grain. The pasture area should be fenced in with woven wire with openings small enough that the young turkeys cannot escape. A shelter large enough to house all the turkeys at once without crowding also should be provided in case of poor weather.

Pigs

Pigs are a great farm addition because they are friendly, easy to care for, and will eat just about anything including kitchen discards such as leftover whey from butter making, food scraps, and excess vegetables not suitable for table use. A pig's growth from birth to market only takes around six months, so they can be raised and sold within one season. This rapid growth and highly varied appetite makes pigs a suitable option for the small farm.

Feeder pigs, or pigs weighing between 40 and 80 pounds, can be purchased directly from breeders or through shows and auction barns. They are generally fairly cheap, from 50 to 90 cents a pound and can be raised to butcher weight of 225 to 250 pounds in five or six months. Housing needs for feeder pigs are minimal, and they are happy in a pen with outdoor access. A concrete pad — at least in the feeding and drinking areas — will make it easier to clean and sanitize your pig palace when getting new pigs. Contrary to legend, pigs are actually clean animals and prefer a well-kept home. They also need a shady spot, watering hole, or cool barn in the summer and a heated shed or barn in the winter.

A typical feeder pig setup includes a three-sided shed with the opening facing toward the south or east to take advantage of sun and to protect against prevailing northerly and westerly winds. A simple V-shaped plywood hut or even a piece of plywood nailed up against a building can provide shelter for your herd from rain and sun during the summer. Allow 25 square feet of space per adult pig, and keep it bedded with dry straw or hay. Shelters on skids have the added advantage of allowing you to easily move the shelter when you move the pigs to a different pasture. A concrete pad will run from the shed to give the pigs an area to get sunlight, fresh air, and exercise. The shed should be bedded with straw or hay, and typically, the pigs will pick an area of the concrete pad to use as a toilet.

In areas with subzero winter temperatures and blizzards, a well-enclosed shed with heat is needed as pigs are susceptible to frostbite. A 12-inch deep straw bed will allow your pigs to build nests to provide themselves with further insulation from very cold temperatures. Monitor the bedding carefully and remove soiled and wet bedding promptly to avoid a buildup of ammonia fumes. In both summer and winter, the shelter should remain dry in wet weather.

If you do not have a building or shed to house pigs, pigs can be kept on pasture during warm weather. Properly constructed fences surrounding an area of underbrush can provide a safe, summer place for pigs. Fences can be constructed of wood, woven wire, hog panels, or electrical fence wire. Pigs will root and will use their noses like a shovel to dig under fences. Digging down into the ground to place a string of chicken wire and installing boards along the base of the fence line can curb this practice. A small pig can

wriggle through 3-by-3-inch gaps and a large 225-pound market pig can rip down fences, so your pen will have to be sturdy to keep the pigs secure and in place.

Pastured pigs will have natural access to vitamins and minerals found in the soil and pasture plants. Typically, these are supplemented in feed mixes purchased at feed stores, but quality varies depending on supplier. Pigs need less pasture per animal than your typical pasture animals. Pasture-raising pigs also eliminates many of the negatives associated with confinement rearing such as tail-biting and manure accumulation, which leads to better sanitation.

The best pasture forage for pigs is alfalfa or clover mixed with grass. The legumes will add needed protein, and feed costs can be up to 20 percent less for pasture-reared pigs than those reared in strict confinement. Plan to stock the pasture at a rate of ten pigs per acre to minimize overgrazing. Another rule is to not pasture the same land two years in a row in order to break the transmission of parasites. See the Ontario County Agricultural Enhancement Board's website for more information on pasturing pigs: **www.fingerlakes agriculture.com/involved/livestock.php**.

Goats

Goats are a fairly easy-to-keep species because they have minimal housing needs. They also eat very little grain but do need good quality hay and pasture. One big advantage of owning goats is that they will eat many of the weeds and brush that cattle will not consume. Goats are curious animals and love to explore their environment with their lips and tongues. They are also smart and will search fences, gates, gate latches, and living quarters for an escape route from confinement. Because of their nimbleness and good sense of balance, they are high climbers and can climb over high fences. Low tree limbs surrounding pens or pastures also provide another escape route for these Houdinis.

Goats are a versatile breed as they can provide both food and fiber. Their meat, especially from the Boer goat, is popular around the world and prized at many foreign food markets. Dairy goats provide milk that can be substituted for cow's milk by people with allergies or lactose intolerance. Goat milk is made into cheese, butter, yogurt, and ice cream and is sought out by high-end chefs and cheese connoisseurs. In terms of fiber, the Angora goat can produce up to 15 pounds of mohair each year, and goats bred for cashmere can yield about 9 ounces of soft cashmere wool each year.

Goats are happy to range about your farm but need shelter from wind, predators, and wet weather. Your geographical location will determine the type of housing your goats need. In dry, arid regions, you need only wind and shade protection. Colder, harsher climates require a sturdier structure to protect from winter winds and wet snow.

Dairy goats need housing and a milking setup that is a bit more elaborate, and you will need a sturdy, well-maintained barn devoted to your dairy herd. To keep this barn as sanitary as possible, no other goats or animals should be housed with the dairy goat herd. The does (female goats) can be kept in two ways:

- Loose housing, which consists of one or two large pens for the goats. This arrangement gives does exercise and social contact, and the manure pack can provide extra warmth in the winter, as it emits some heat and insulates from the ground. The big disadvantage of a loose housing situation is it is hard to maintain the manure pack with a dry upper layer, and hay must be fed above the ground to lessen the transmission of parasites.

- Individual pen or tie-stall housing has higher initial costs due to construction, and it can deprive the does of exercise and social contact. It is easier to keep individual pens clean.

Bucks (male goats) also should be given their own shelter with the same standard as the housing for the does and young stock and with either option, access to the outside is important

The milking area for the does should be separate from the stable and needs to have a concrete floor. An 8-by-8-foot area will be sufficient for milking one or two does at a time. A drain also should be placed in the concrete to allow for thorough cleaning of the milking area. If your plans include selling the milk to the public, please check with your state milk board for the particular requirements for the milking area. It will need to pass state inspection before the milk can be sold. Of course, if your family is consuming the milk, you still will want to have a clean, pest-free milking area to ensure they consume quality milk.

Does are trained to be milked on a milking platform that is generally 18 inches wide by 3.5 feet long. These stands are mounted on stilts or legs that raise the platform 15 to 18 inches from the floor. This will help facilitate milking, and a trained goat readily will leap onto the stand, particularly if she is routinely fed her grain ration at the same time.

Other necessary equipment in the milking area is a hot water heater, a double sink, a rack for drying and storing milking equipment, and a refrigeration source. You will need the hot water and sinks to clean and sanitize your milking equipment. A regular refrigerator can be used for family milk consumption. If you have a larger herd or plan to sell to the public or a milk processor, you will need to invest in a cooler or a bulk tank. The walls and ceilings should be free from drips and should not allow moisture to condense. To help combat moisture problems, adequate ventilation should be maintained. Insulation also can help prevent condensation from forming during cold weather. Electricity to the building is a must in order to run exhaust fans and to provide light.

For more information on goat (and sheep) farming, check out the University of Maryland's Small Ruminant Page: **www.sheepandgoat.com**.

Sheep

Sheep make a wonderful addition to the farmstead and can be a valuable tool for weed control. They provide fiber and meat, and for a small farm enterprise, sheep fit well into a low-input farming system because they need minimal housing if lambing coincides with warm spring weather.

Starting out with a small group of ewes (ten to 20) and a ram is an excellent way to enter into sheep farming. While not as common as dairy goats, some breeds of sheep are used for dairying. The requirements for the sheep dairy barn and pens are the same as for goats.

CASE STUDY: RAISING WOOL-LESS SHEEP

Catherine's for Lamb & Pfennig Farms
kpfennig@bektel.com
www.catherinesforlamb.com
Driscoll, ND

Catherine and Kent Pfennig raise Katahdin Hair Sheep — a wool-less breed of sheep in Driscoll, North Dakota. This breed of sheep was developed in the U.S. as a meat breed of sheep. They require no shearing. The Katahdin sheep also produces consistently high quality meat.

The Pfennig flock now consists of 300 breeding ewes. The meat from the lambs is processed for restaurant and retail markets. They also directly market their meat to consumers through their website, local contacts, and via CSA.

Catherine is originally from New Zealand, where she grew up eating lamb, but that was not the only reason they decided to raise sheep. They had a weed problem in their pastures. The pastures also had alfalfa, so they could not use an herbicide to kill the leaves as it would also kill the alfalfa. So they decided to use sheep to control the weed problem.

They started with 16 ewes and chose a wool-less breed, as it is hard to find a person to shear the sheep in their area. They use rotational grazing techniques on their farm to manage their pastures and to minimize any soil erosion issues.

Catherine did a lot of research before marketing her lamb products. She had to search hard to find a meat processor that could slaughter the animals to her specifications. She was able to use a grant from the commerce department to help with product development and marketing. Also, membership in associations such as Pride of Dakota and the International Association of Culinary Professionals (IACP) has been a great help in guiding and encouraging her to market her products.

Catherine recommends that beginning farmers focus on quality and consistency. She believes tenacity and confidence in the venture, a love of the land, and a desire to have quality of life over getting rich quick are the keys to successful farm life. More practically, she recommends the beginning sheep farmer purchase an ATV, a tractor, and an electronet — a portable electric fence. They suggest that beginners investigate beginner farmer loans but have another source of income as you get established and grow your customer base.

Beef Cattle

In general, healthy adult beef cattle in good condition can live outside provided they have a windblock to protect from winter wind chills. A thick stand of trees, the side of a farm building, or a solid-sided fence to protect from prevailing winds will help around the farmyard. A covered shed will give them protection from chilling rain or wet, heavy snow.

Young calves or a pregnant cow near delivery date should be provided with a shed or a barn to escape bad weather. The barn should be ventilated to eliminate buildup of ammonia fumes and circulate fresh air. Bedding material, such as straw or corn stalks, should be maintained so there is always a dry layer on top. It can be allowed to build up until you are able to clean the pen more thoroughly provided there are no wet areas.

If you are starting with an established farm, be sure to repair or remove broken fence panels, bent steel posts, or rusty metal from pens, corrals, and pastures. Cows can be impaled by or entangled in these items or escape through a gap in a downed fence.

A popular and relatively inexpensive way to raise beef cattle and young calves is on pasture. A good technique to practice is rotational grazing, which can extend the grazing season and give you more grass yield per acre of pasture than simply allowing the cattle to roam freely over all your available pastureland.

The principle behind rotational grazing is fairly simple. Cattle are placed in a paddock and allowed to graze until the grass is eaten down to an approximate remainder of 4 to 6 inches. Then, the cattle are moved to the next paddock, eat that grass, and continue to move on until the final paddock is grazed. By the end of this cycle the first paddock should have new grass ready for the cattle to eat. The key to success with rotational grazing is to move the cattle before they are allowed to graze the grass too short. This way the grass will recover faster and be ready for the herd when it comes back. To determine if pasture raised beef or dairy cattle will work for your farm, review the National Sustainable Agriculture Information Service on-line publication: **http://attra.ncat.org**.

Setting up a rotational grazing plan will take some planning. To start, grab a pencil and notebook, and sketch out an outline of your available pastureland. Divide the pasture into at least six, three-acre paddocks. With adequate rainfall and water sources, a one- to three-acre area can support one beef cow and calf pair or one dairy cow on a moderately intensive rotational grazing plan. Once you have your paddocks planned, you will need to plan your fences. A three-strand electrical fence or a woven-wire fence with a top line of electric wire will hold your cattle in the appropriate paddocks. Be sure to include gates or alleyways to allow the cattle to move from paddock to paddock. Installing the fences is a labor-intensive job so give yourself time to put everything in and make sure the fence posts have time to set before stringing fence or bringing in cattle.

To be successful, each paddock will need a water source. You can use natural sources such as ponds, but using simple irrigation pipe will provide a more reliable and fresher source of water. This pipe can be purchased at general farm supply stores in 50-foot spools of black plastic pipe. It is connected together with simple plastic fittings to make a fairly inexpensive water supply. The watering system can be placed the spring before implementing the practice. It does not need to be buried, except at gates or where cattle may trample or cut it with their hooves. Remember to drain the pipe before freezing weather. Generally, paddocks can share pipes to save on expenses, so try a few sketches to make sure you do not use excessive pipes. A portable stock tank, available at farm supply stores, is sufficient to hold the water.

Dairy Cattle

Becoming a small-scale dairy farmer will take hard, physical work and dedication as cows need to be milked twice daily, seven days a week, when they are in production. You also will need to be a savvy business owner to keep production costs down while making sure your herd produces enough milk to cover costs.

Dairy cattle are typically housed in barns. They are animals that thrive on routine and usually will have a favorite spot in the barn. Most small-scale dairy farmers will use stanchions (devices that latch around the cow's neck) or a tie-stall (where the cattle are chained to the stall via a neck chain) to hold the cows while milking. Milk sold to the public or to milk-handling plants is strictly regulated by state boards. There are also minimum barn and equipment requirements, which vary by state.

Some farmers choose to leave their cattle in the barn continuously, occasionally letting them out if they have stopped milking during their dry period or for just a few hours a day while the barn is being cleaned. It is healthier for cattle to be able to spend time exercising, and they can be maintained well on pasture. A rotational grazing plan, exactly like beef cattle, can be used with dairy cattle.

The main requirement for dairy cattle is to have dry teats and a clean place to lie down. The udder needs to remain clean and can be contaminated quickly by manure if a clean top layer of bedding is not provided. Dairy cattle that are allowed access to a pasture should not be able to walk into standing water or a river as some waters carry microorganisms that can cause serious udder infections.

Good milking procedure, fine-tuned milking machines, and a clean environment should eliminate most cases of mastitis, or mammary gland infection. All people who milk and care for a dairy cow should be trained to properly prepare the milking cow for milking and how to spot signs of mastitis. Mastitis is the biggest health problem facing dairy cows, as it decreases milk production and can make the milk undrinkable or unsalable.

Dairy cattle and have the same general feed requirements as beef cattle, but since they are expending energy producing milk, they will need higher quantities. Most dairy cattle produce 6 to 7 gallons of milk a day, and they will eat around 100 pounds of feed a day including hay, grass, silage, and grain. The better they are fed, the better milk they will produce. Dairy cows also need access to water at all times.

Grain usually is fed to the cattle while they are in their stalls and being milked. Larger dairies will have a machine to mix and grind all the feeds together into a single product. This way the cow will consume all feeds, get proper nutrition, and not just pick out the feed she finds tastiest. The cost of a TMR mixer, though, is high for a small farmer. You will need to mix the feed by hand before feeding it to each cow.

Chapter 6

Researching Your Markets and Selling Your Products

dentifying the best place to sell your product is a bit of a chicken-and-the-egg problem. You must first know who will buy your product and how to reach them. To know this, though, you will have to understand your fellow sellers or your competition and what type of products they are selling within your market. This in-formation might affect they type of products you are selling, so you might end up with different cus-tomers than you originally antici-pated. You see how this can be a bit circular? So, to give you a starting point, this chapter will focus on po-tential competitors and selling ven-ues. The next chapter will talk about identifying your customer and dis-cuss marketing techniques to reach them. These two chapters work to-

gether, so be sure to read each thoroughly before you settle completely on your product line.

The term "the market" is thrown around within every industry. It can refer to broad-ranging forces such as inflation or stagnation. It can relate to forces as small as bad weather closing down your selling venue for the day. As a seller, the market will influence your actions but you, in turn, can find ways to put these powerful forces to work for your business. Your market not only includes customers but also your competitors selling the same or similar products. They want their slice of the pie just as badly as you do, so success lies in understanding what drives the market, identifying potential problems or roadblocks, and developing solutions for using the market to your advantage. This is one case where knowledge truly is power. The more you understand about these things, the better prepared you will be to compete successfully.

Competition

Unless you have created a truly unique or one-of-a-kind product, competition exists in every business, in every niche, and for every product offering. If it does not exist when you begin, you can be sure someone else eventually will copy your product. A thorough understanding of the competitors you face should be the basis of determining your product offerings. By knowing what products share your selling space, you can find a way to differentiate yourself and stand out from the crowd. This differentiation may be on price, in delivery terms, on quality, or simply on good customer service. Researching your competition will help you find holes in their product line waiting to be filled.

As a produce farmer, you have competition from numerous angles. Within the produce type, consumers can choose to buy from the next sales booth at the farmers' market, from alternate farmers' markets or CSAs, from supermarkets or surplus stores, or even grow their own garden. Consumers also might prefer frozen or canned versions of your offerings or a different type of produce within that variety. For instance, a shopper may be just as happy to have romaine lettuce instead of red leaf lettuce for his salad if the alternative item is better quality or offered at a significantly lower price.

As a meat and dairy farmer, you face competition from supermarkets, meat markets, butchers, hunters, mail-order foods, and online ordering. Many people have long-standing attachments to their butcher or meat-market or they are determined to get the lowest price possible. Often, people choose their meat supplier based only on perceived safety of the food — either in how the animal was raised or how the meat is processed.

As a small producer you cannot possibly be everything to every customer — that is the job of the big box stores. You can, however, become really good at your specific niche and find enough customers to turn a nice profit. You can choose to diversify just enough to reach a little wider circle of customers, or you can find a gap in the selling market that is easy for you to fill. Again, knowing your market well will give you quick entry into sales and long-lasting staying power with your customers.

Assessing competitors

As a small business owner, it is easy to overestimate who your true competition really is. Casting too wide a net in an effort to beat the competition often results in you spending a lot of extra time and money without much return on investment. For example, if you are planning to sell exclusively at farmers' markets, then your primary competition is the person down the row selling the same item or even the farmers' market in another part of town. Supermarkets or grocery stores are your secondary competition — spending money to reach the grocery store customer will not have as big an effect as targeting farmers' market customers. If you are selling produce to large wholesalers or grocery stores, your competition is the other producer selling the same product and not the grocery store down the street or the person at the farmers' market. Your customer in this case is the grocery store buyer, and he or she must be convinced that your product is the best. Of course, every market has some overlap, and it will not hurt your business to keep a presence in all potential selling venues. Identifying and focusing your major efforts on the right market will be the most effective use of your marketing dollars and effort.

Assessing your competition is a bit like being a secret agent. Go undercover and shop the farmers' market, or ask your supermarket where they get their products. Look at everything that goes into the sale — presentation, variety, quality, price, customer service, and location. Are there gaps in any of the areas? Are there sellers who are doing a great job? Ask your fellow shoppers what they think about the offerings. Research the particular selling venue by asking the sponsor questions such as how many vendors are signed up, if there is other local competition, if the sponsor is looking for something different, or if there are any future plans for expansion. These notes and answers will all be clues to your position in the market and will help you narrow down your customer base. Once you know your base, you can develop the plan that best fits your product and choose the most appropriate selling venue to reach your target customer.

Farmers' Markets

The number of farmers' markets in the United States has been growing exponentially since the mid-1990s due to increasing demand for farm-fresh produce. Many consumers shop farmers' markets to support local businesses, find organic, unique, or fresh produce, and to connect with like-minded people.

For a budding farmer, these markets provide the simplest market entry point and are a good way to establish a customer base and reputation quickly. Your presence at farmers' markets will introduce your product line to a wide range of people you would not encounter otherwise. You also will have an opportunity to convert these people into regular customers who might be willing to come to events at your farm, get home delivery, or sign up for a subscription service.

Farmers' markets are also reliable and flexible selling venues, providing an outlet for selling just about any type or amount of hand-grown or hand-made items. Depending on local regulations, you will find people selling everything from fresh produce to honey to handmade soaps to fresh-churned butter. You also will have flexibility in pricing — you can set your own prices and choose to sell by the item, by the pound, or discount your rates for bulk purchases. Be prepared, though, for days when attendance is low or bargain hunters come to your booth looking for deep discounts or special deals.

Farmers' markets also can be found in every size town, including small rural towns and large metropolitan areas. Many of the larger markets move the sales to an indoor venue when the weather is cold. Many markets charge an entry or table fee and expect you to be at the market each week. To locate a farmers' market in your area, contact the USDA's Agricultural Marketing Service at **www.ams.usda.gov/farmersmarkets**.

A few tips for choosing and selling at a farmers' market:

- Sometimes gaining an advantage at a farmers' market is as simple as being the first to set up. Be prepared to get there early and stay late.
- There can be a wide variance in the quality of farmers' markets. The first one you find may not be a good fit for you and your products.
- Look for a market located in a busy, centralized place, and be sure it is well publicized. Do no undercut the other sellers. Similar, fair market practices create an environment that encourages more customers. Furthermore, if your prices are dramatically lower than a fellow farmer's, consumers may discount the quality of your products.
- Always have plenty of change — bring at least $100 in ones and fives.
- Bring twice as many bags as you think you will need.

- Keep your table or stand looking neat and bountiful. Keep all your baskets full and give samples when possible.
- Stay standing or seated on a high stool so that you are at eye-level with patrons. It makes you more approachable.
- Make eye contact, smile, and be genuinely friendly, as making a personal connection is important.
- Invest in a large banner with the name of your farm, your logo, and any information that might be important to consumers, such as "certified organic."
- Bring a scale, calculator, cash box, pen and paper, and recipes.
- Do not be afraid to have a gimmick, even if it is just selling water.
- Label prices clearly, either on a large chalkboard or individual crates.

All these practices will help you draw customers to your product, but remember the best selling practice is to offer the best quality product possible.

On-Farm Sales or Agritourism

On-farm sales can be a promising opportunity for your farm, depending on its location. Easy access off a main road or proximity to a town will encourage people to make the trek out to your farm. That does not mean that a remote location rules your farm out completely; it just requires more creativity.

Many farms have moved toward creating their farm as a destination for a fun family outing. Corn mazes, pumpkin patches, haunted houses, or pick-your-own packages are unique experiences for many town kids and families are willing to pay a good price for these experiences. Some small farms also have expanded into hosting weddings, retreats, camps, and other tourism-related activities. The trick is to think about what differentiates your farm, what skills you have, and how you can capitalize on these things. For more information on agritourism in your area, explore your local government initiatives, festivals, and state tourism websites and brochures.

Bringing a lot of visitors to your farm can create problems and might be subject to special licensure. Check with local government agencies regarding any special permits or licenses related to the activity you are planning. These permits can be costly and potentially can eat into the profits you would reap from the venture. Logistically, too, be sure your farm, your family, and your neighbors can handle an influx of people for busy weekend events. These folks might interfere with your daily chores, spook your animals, and clog your road with parked cars. Check your insurance policy carefully to be sure you have the proper coverage. Remember, too, that with a home-based business such as this, you will never be "closed." People will stop by at all hours, on any given day, and may even come to your farm on holidays or busy harvest days.

CASE STUDY: TAKING ADVANTAGE OF LOCAL BUSINESS OPPORTUNITIES

Waheed (Wally) Rabbani
Rabbani Orchards
Grimsby, Ontario, Canada

Waheed (Wally) Rabbani has owned and operated Rabbani Orchards since1990. He has a small orchard with many different types of fruits including cherries, apricots, peaches, plums, pears, apples, strawberries, and raspberries. While Canada may be thought of as a harsh climate for these tender fruits, the orchard is in the Niagara region of Ontario with a microclimate conducive to growing these fruits.

Rabbani decided to enter into the farming business as a long-term investment because of its income potential and eventually as an avenue to retirement. He also wanted to live in a rural area so he could get away from the big city and out to the fresh, clean air. However, because the orchard was located close enough to densely populated urban areas, he has been able to take advantage of busy farmers' markets. He sells fresh fruit as well as value-added products, such as apple cider and preserves.

His biggest challenge has been handling the ripe, fresh fruit. The fruit requires careful picking and handling and coordination to make sure that each fruit is picked at the right time so it can be kept fresh without too much refrigeration. This has also become his most successful marketing technique as his fresh, ripe fruit helped him establish a dedicated and loyal clientele.

He also has spent a lot of time actively marketing his products. He listed his farm in farm catalogues and put up signs to advertise his farm and produce. He frequently updates his telephone message recording to notify callers when fruits were available.

The farm keeps Rabbani quite busy throughout the year. Wintertime chores include pruning trees, maintaining and repairing equipment, and furthering his knowledge through study and seminars on fruit farming. He even has vacationed to warmer climates to learn different farming methods.

Springtime farm chores include more pruning, fertilizing, cultivating, and spraying. Summertime brings an explosion of work: more spraying, grass mowing, and picking, sorting, packing, and marketing fruit. Fall brings more grass mowing, spraying, and continuing fruit harvesting and marketing along with attending farm fairs and conferences. He hires employees as needed for farm chores and fruit picking.

Despite all the hard work, Rabbani greatly enjoys managing his farm. It gives him great satisfaction to see the results of his hard labor — large, healthy produce free of bugs and disease. He also enjoys seeing his customers at the farmers' markets happy to purchase and pay a fair price for his fruit.

According to Rabbani the challenges facing small acreage fruit farmers are a shortage of local help and the rising costs of farm inputs. Farmers are putting in longer hours for the same amount of pay, and this is leading to financial hardship. Large supermarkets are also a big competition for the small orchard farm due to their accessibility for customers and cheap imports of offshore produce. Rabbani feels the only way to combat this competition is by maintaining high quality and freshness of products at the farmers' markets. This quality will ensure a loyal customer base.

Subscription or Community Supported Agriculture

A recent trend in farmer-direct sales is the subscription service or community supported agriculture (CSA) membership. CSAs are basically a marketing method that requires customers to pay an up-front fee for a share of the farmer's yield. If the crop does well, the customer gets a lot of produce. If the crop fails, the customer gets little or no product. The fee is nonrefundable so the customer essentially is taking on some of the risk of the farm. The customer, too, will share in the bounty of extra-high yields without being expected to pay in any more money. Some CSAs also offer members discounts on their shares if they commit to volunteering on the farm a certain number of hours per week.

Typically, members get a weekly or biweekly "basket" of goods produced on the farm — the products vary widely by farm, and the offerings are determined at the beginning of the season. Members usually come to the farm to pick up their shares every week, providing an opportunity for the

farmer to sell other products not typically included in a share, such as a limited yield of berries that week or an extra loaf of bread. You must be located within a reasonable driving distance to your customers. If not, offer home delivery or arrange for deliveries to a central distribution site.

Before offering a CSA, it is important to have well-established and reliable production. Be sure to sell the right amount of shares your farm can support — leaving enough produce for other needs such as your family, your animals, or other selling venues. Your offerings in a CSA depend greatly on your farm and your experience. Most subscriptions offer a seasonal variety and can include value-added or unique items such as eggs, bread, honey, nuts, grains, or meat and poultry. Your location can make or break you. If you are far off, it may be difficult to find members, and it may be impractical for you to travel weekly to where the majority of your CSA members are located. Carefully consider the costs and risks involved. Even CSA members may not feel distance is an issue at first but eventually may find it inconvenient enough to decide not to renew their CSA membership.

Advantages

- Allows you to share the risk of a bad season or crop failure
- Fosters community relationships and provides a foundation for future product ventures
- Built-in demand for your product and easier delivery method than a farmers' market

Disadvantages

- Shared reward of high yields — be sure to designate which harvests fall under the CSA agreement.
- Getting customers to continue with the CSA typically requires involvement from you such as a newsletter to help members feel connected to your farm. If your CSA is not at least partially labor-based, you have to know that you have enough hands to do the extra work involved with a CSA, such as packaging and delivery.

For more information on joining or forming your own CSA, visit your local library or visit the North Carolina Cooperative Extension website for Growing Small Farms at **www.ces.ncsu.edu**. This website offers a helpful guide to starting and running a CSA, including how to organize your structure, set your share price, connect with customers, and more. Additionally, the USDA website has a wealth of current CSA information, data, and assistance for those looking to start or manage this type of farm.

Wholesale

If the idea of direct-to-consumer selling does not appeal to you, you may consider supplying your products to businesses on a wholesale basis. Restaurants, particularly higher-end restaurants, are an extremely lucrative market as they have the profit margins to support purchasing the freshest ingredients. Wholesale sales to restaurants have a minimum of a 10-percent higher return than other wholesale counterparts. Furthermore, there is a growing insistence for locally grown produce and animal products, and each restaurant markets these heavily.

It can be difficult to establish a connection with a restaurant because they are unsure you will be able to deliver consistent quality and volume. Encourage these relationships by researching those with specialty products and bringing samples for the chef and the restaurant manager to try. Be sure to include a brochure that lists estimates for what your yields will be, how you can ensure consistent quality, what you will do if you fail to have the volume they request, and delivery logistics. You also could consider providing an updated list to the restaurant weekly as to what items will become available that week. Private or large institutions, such as schools, prisons, diet clinics, and nursing homes also may be candidates for wholesale services.

Advantages

- Assurance of knowing all or part of your product offering is already intended for an established buyer
- Opportunity to expand your product offerings to complement the restaurant's needs, meaning more stable sales for you

Disadvantages

- Most restaurants buy in limited quantities; sometimes the sales will not justify the frequent deliveries.

- Most restaurants will want fresh produce; this may be difficult when trying to sell animal production, such as beef or lamb.
- Most restaurants like to mix it up a bit, but on their terms. This means that you will have to be very flexible in what you provide.

Internet

Although frequently overlooked by many farmers, the Internet offers many opportunities for the savvy farming operation. As a small business, it is a good idea to maintain your own website so you can reach a wider range of customers. Just by posting your latest product offerings, directions to your farm, and ideas on how to use your products, you might gain new customers who quickly will become old customers. Website design and maintenance can be expensive but many low-cost and easy-to-use alternatives exist for do-it-yourselfers.

You also can use social networking websites or set up a blog to keep the buzz going about your farm, post upcoming events, or even list items for sale. Auction sites such as eBay® or classifieds sites such as Craigslist are great sites for selling unique or seasonal products. Through these sites, you basically will be running a mail-order business, but your product is fresh produce. Be aware, though, of shipping rules to other countries regarding natural products, many of which are not allowed to pass the border.

Consider listing your farm on a website such as Local Harvest℠ found at **www.localharvest.org**, which acts a sort of watering hole for farmers, CSA subscriptions, agricultural events, and the like. They provide you with a profile page and a secure system to take credit card payments. Make sure to list your farm with organizations that maintain websites of local attractions or small businesses, as this is basically free advertising.

How to Get Paid

Most customers will pay you on the spot for your product or on a biweekly or monthly basis such as with a CSA. However, in some cases such as when you are selling to a wholesaler, you will be expected to invoice the customer after delivery. You might also have online payments that you will run through a service such as PayPal®. Whatever arrangement works for you is fine as long as your customers understand the terms, and you accurately track and account for staggered or delayed payments.

For immediate payments, cash is always the best choice. At most, direct-to-consumer markets people expect to pay in cash so be sure to have plenty of small bills on hand to make change. Some markets now are allowing purchases through the USDA Supplemental Assistance Nutrition Program (SNAP.) In most cases, your market manager will handle the specifics of this program and provide you with a card reader or give scrips or tokens to customers that they will use at your booth. Check with your market representative or visit the USDA website for more information. Accepting SNAP payments can be a benefit to your market as it attracts new customers that otherwise would be unable to shop with you. Additionally, it provides a community service for those looking to buy fresh, wholesome food with their food assistance money.

Another recently introduced smartphone credit-card reader allows you to accept credit cards as payment on the spot, even from rural locations. These small plug-in readers attach to your smartphone or Internet-ready tablet; you just swipe your customer's card, and the money goes right to your account. These readers are available through various companies such as **squareup.com** or **payanywhere.com**™. These companies typically will send you a free plug-in and charge a small percentage of each sale's total.

Check first with your own credit card company or wireless provider and be sure to select a reputable company with low fees.

For ongoing billing or long-term payment arrangements, the best way to keep your accounts in order is to create an invoice or bill to send to your customer. An invoice makes your business much more official, provides a written trail for both you and your customer to refer to, and gives you a way to track your sales over time. The invoice should state what was delivered, when it was delivered, the per-unit price, and the total amount owed. Be sure to include your contact information on the invoice so your customer can send you payment. Be sure your invoice states that payment is due upon receipt, and spell out the payment methods you prefer. Most word-processing programs offer a simple invoice template, and office supply stores sell receipt books perfect for writing out invoices. Most online billing sites also offer invoicing services with which you can create invoices and billing statements to send electronically.

If you are selling things online, use a payment service such as PayPal, and make sure the payment clears your bank before you ship the item. State clearly in your listings or website that you only accept payment through these arrangements and will not ship the item until the payment has cleared. Larger sites such as eBay have feedback ratings for buyers, too, and you can leave negative feedback if the sale does not go well.

Sadly, a customer occasionally will try to avoid paying. Your first step should be to make sure the customer is satisfied with your product. If not, do what you can to make it right, but do not expect to get paid extra. If they are just trying to avoid payment, you do not have a lot of recourse, as collection agencies can be quite costly. Be sure, though, to cross these customers off your list because they probably will try to skip payment again.

Chapter 7

Marketing: How Do I Get the Word Out Effectively?

For a small farmer, having a good marketing strategy is as important as having a green thumb. You can grow the tastiest tomato and package it in the prettiest container but without a customer, you are just a gardener. The final step in your production process is a marketing strategy that reaches the most customers for the lowest cost. Marketing also builds your brand and establishes your image in the marketplace, often making the sale before the customer even sees your produce. Developing a thoughtful, well-executed marketing strategy is critical to long-term success. You do not have to spend a lot of money to market your business, and many free or almost-free alternatives exist for the small farmer. It is important, however, to stay in control of your message and take an active role in marketing efforts.

Developing a Marketing Strategy

Marketing is more than placing an ad in the weekly paper or hanging a poster at your grocery store. A true marketing plan grows out of a full marketing strategy that identifies the customer, determines ways to appeal to this customer, and then outlines the methods to get your message out. Sometimes called the five P's of marketing, your strategy should address all five areas: people or customers, price, packaging, place of sales, and promotion or public relations. There are no hard and fast rules here, but these five segments allow you to consider fully the factors present in your selling arena. This consideration and review will ensure you maximize every marketing opportunity available to your business, your brand, and your specific product. Your marketing strategy is also an ever-changing creature, review it regularly to make sure it is working well, and you are not missing any opportunities.

People

This category comes first for a good reason: Without customers or people to buy your product, you do not have a business. The group of people most likely to buy your product is called your target market or your demographic. Defining your target market can be incredibly scientific and large companies spend millions of dollars each year on demographic research. As a small producer you will not need this level of review. In most cases you can assess your target market by watching customer behavior at sales locations, asking a few questions of shoppers and other businesspeople, and listening to that inner voice telling you what works and what does not work. A marketing plan can be changed easily, adjusted, and tweaked if it is not working. Any research into demographics ultimately needs the answers to these questions:

- Who is my customer? This description can include gender, age or age range, income or discretionary spending, attitude or bias, distance from your product, and how they plan to use the product.

- What motivates my customer? Is it price, convenience, quality, ease-of-use, vendor loyalty, or impulse purchases?

- How does my competition reach this demographic? Do they offer promotions or freebies, is their packaging nicer, is their price better, or is your competition missing the mark?

As you gather data, think like a customer. What is a customer looking for in a product? You need to understand what drives your potential customer's buying decisions. Be brutally honest with yourself as you review your product — if there is anything wrong, customers will see it. Look for what is right, too. What are the biggest benefits of your product and how can these be highlighted so you will reach that target market. For example, are your customers looking for organic products? If your product is organically certified, include that claim in your packaging or signage. These answers also can lead you into product changes or enhancements to better meet a potential need.

Existing customers are also part of your demographic and are the easiest segment of your market to reach. Nurturing or growing sales within this existing base could be all you need to meet your goals, and you might not need to court new buyers. If you have personal contact with your repeat customers, ask them what they like, what they do not like, and what they would like to see added or changed. Make sure your customers are satisfied and if not, do whatever is necessary to regain their business. Happy customers are truly the best advertising. Do not become so overzealous with finding new customers that you start to neglect your existing base.

Price

The range of pricing methods varies widely by industry, by competition, and by individual business goals. Selecting a price too high can push you out of the market, while choosing a price too low can make customers think your product is inferior. Some farms choose to set their prices at the average price of their competitors thinking this will allow them to compete on an equal footing for quality. Other farmers try to undercut their competitors' pricing as a way to win the market on price alone. Some also choose to adjust pricing in the opposite direction, charging more for their items as a way to infer a superior quality. In some cases this upward pricing is warranted such as with rare, organic, or specialty products.

Breakeven analysis is another popular pricing method in which you calculate the amount of income needed to break even — or satisfy expenses related to that product. Prices then are set based on projected sales with an additional percentage of desired profit included. For example, if it costs you $1000 to bring your crop to market, then you would need to sell this entire crop for $1300 to see a 30-percent profit. Expenses or input costs include everything needed from start to finish such as fuel to till the land, seed and fertilizer, materials, marketing, labor costs, insurance, legal fees, and booth rental. At the end of the season, anything over your input costs becomes your profit or your salary. This method is easier to use once you have been raising and selling product for awhile. In the beginning, you will not know all your input costs or projected sales levels until the season is over.

On a small-scale you will know right away if your prices are not right. If you are watching customers pass by to consistently buy from another booth, your prices might be too high. If you sell out before anyone else at the farmers' market, your prices might be too low. Of course, your customer may or may not be choosing you for other reasons, but these can be good indicators of a need for price adjustments. You cannot, however, raise your prices significantly mid-season or start charging wholesalers a higher price, but it is important to track these things for next season. You should at least make enough to meet your expenses, make a reasonable profit, but still appeal to your target market.

> **HOW TO:** Use a Loss Leader Strategy for Pricing. Big grocery stores have known for years that if you lure in customers with a ridiculously low-priced item, they will fill up their baskets with other more profitable merchandise. This strategy also can work for a small seller. Can you add a product to your line with low input costs that can be sold at a low price? This is a great way to bring in new customers or get existing customers to buy more products. Just make sure you have the supplies to meet demand.

Packaging

Packaging strongly affects the subconscious decisions buyers make and changes the way a customer views your products. In the food industry this is even more important because customers want to know your product is tasty, safe, and worth the money. This is one of the primary reasons supermarkets coat produce with wax — the produce looks more appetizing because the color and shine are enhanced. Packaging also relates

Handmade soaps and lotions for sale at a local farmers market

to the way your products are displayed, protected, and packaged after the sale. Clean vegetables displayed nicely or packaged carefully will show your customers that your products are worth the money. Conversely, piles of dirty vegetables lying on the ground or in the hot sun are not very appetizing to a potential buyer.

Expensive packaging can also bump your product into the premium category. Consider the masterful marketing of the premium food and gift company, Harry & David®. Through their beautiful packaging and easy online ordering, this company has made a huge business out of selling ordinary fruits, nuts, and more. Pears are probably their most famous product, and people willingly pay more than $5 per pound for these pears, several times the market rate. The pears are wrapped individually in paper, with separators between each one, and placed on a bed of decorative straw. While these pears are good, they are no better than a fresh pear off a tree. Harry and David have differentiated themselves by unique packaging that invokes a feeling that these pears are truly something special.

Another packaging strategy frequently used by successful farmers is rustic packaging: things such as the old-fashioned stall at the farmers' market, the handwritten signs, the woven baskets, and the brown paper bags. Without realizing it, many farmers adopt this packaging out of convenience and what is available. However, doing so emphasizes that the products come from a farmer with a face, rather than an anonymous bin at the market, thereby differentiating your products. Having a human presence is extremely important to a small farm because it allows customers to associate your produce with the hard work and care you put into your products. Should you choose this type of packaging, do not be afraid to amp it up a bit — add a large chalkboard with available selections and prices written on it or provide brown paper tote bags for purchases.

Packaging also provides an opportunity to build a brand for your farm. Using bags or other packaging printed with your name and logo will reinforce your brand recognition and lead customers to seek out your products. You also will gain some free advertising as your customers carry their bags around the market. *Developing your name, logo, and brand will be discussed later in this chapter.*

Place

Knowing your customers' buying habits will help you choose the most appropriate selling venue. For example, if you are aiming for the fresh- and organic-seeking customer, a farmers' market will be the best choice for you. If you want to sell your entire harvest in one delivery, choose a wholesaler or supermarket owner. Distance to delivery is also something to consider as hauling your wares to far-off locations might gain more customers but cost you more in fuel and time on the road. Review your choice of selling venues critically. Does the market get good traffic and have a wide variety of sellers, or will you be fighting over the same customer? Does your product fit well into the mix but still offer something different? Are the booth association fees within your budget? Is the market open during the seasons you will have product available? Compare relative profit margins between selling venues to ensure that you are getting the most for your products.

Promotion

Promotions happen any time a price is reduced or something more is provided for the same price. Promotions can include everything from a buy-one-get-one-free to a free shopping bag with purchase to taste samples. Some farmers offer incentives or loyalty rewards programs such as a frequent purchaser discount or a discount on  product prices if bought on a subscription basis. You can design the promotion to fit your customer, your product, and your bottom line.

Promotions can be used to reduce levels of produce such as ripe strawberries that need to be sold quickly before they go bad or to promote a new product such as an exotic vegetable or a line of jams. Many buyers will patronize companies that offer promotions over those who do not, even if they are not buying the item on special. Getting a customer in front of your products through a free offer often can lead to additional sales, which in turn can build into a loyal customer. Just make sure the product you are offering free is high quality and properly showcases your brand.

CASE STUDY:
THE EXPERTS' EXPERTS

Mike Jorgenson
Kathy Draeger
Clinton, MN

Mike Jorgenson and Kathy Draeger have come back to the Jorgenson family farm to delve into sustainable, diversified farming. Mike has a deep history with the farm, as he and his father had a dairy herd for decades. He farmed with his father for ten years before going back to college and earning his degree in agronomy and plant genetics.

Kathy is the Minnesota statewide director of the University of Minnesota Regional Sustainable Development Partnerships and is a key to recreating the local food system as well as setting the agenda for sustainable community development. They are both very knowledgeable in what it takes to make a small farm work and working with local markets.

They have 320 acres of land to manage, and their short-term goal is to turn 80 acres into organic production — a three-year process. During this conversion time there are many things to consider. Since weed control using traditional sprays is not allowed, Mike thinks a crop of alfalfa might be the best bet for controlling weeds. When the farm is certified organic, he hopes to grow seed crops and perennials, which have a higher market value than traditional crops. They also will use money from the Environmental Quality Incentives Program (EQIP) to fence in 60 acres for a rotational grazing program for their cattle. Another 30 acres will be returned to wetlands to help the environment.

Right now they have five registered Dexter cattle that will be placed into the grazing program. As the program progresses, they will add to their herd. They are enthusiastic about the rotational grazing program as a low-input way to farm the land. They are realistic about the high costs of inputs for farms; cash rents and land prices are very high as is the price of equipment. As Mike sees it, the high land prices are killing young farmers. A similar thing happened in the 80s, when land and input prices were high, leading to a market collapse that drove many farmers out of the business.

Eventually, they hope to raise grass-finished beef and plan to explore using sugar turnips to finish the cattle instead of corn and silage. Kathy also would like to process grain into flour and oatmeal. Right now they participate in the local farmers' market, and Kathy found her freshly ground flour to be a big hit with customers. They also market frozen free-range chickens and fresh eggs from the farm.

One big problem they have encountered is the lack of a local market. They live in a sparsely populated county far away from any largely populated areas. This lack of a market eventually will necessitate some creative marketing on their part, probably to institutions in the area, like schools, hospitals, and nursing homes.

They caution that the beginning farmer has to market his or her farm and its products aggressively. Having a diversified farm is very hard work. Beginning farmers should take advantage of the available government programs, such as EQIP through the National Resources Conservation Service.

Despite all of the daunting obstacles, the Jorgenson family is determined to find a way to make it work.

Writing Your Marketing Plan

The answers you find through developing your strategy will lead you into creating a marketing plan. This does not have to be a huge, formal document — it is just a way for you to gather your thoughts, review the data from your research, and plan how you will use this information to build your business. Many people choose to make a short-term marketing plan that covers the coming year or season and a long-range marketing plan that goes out five years or so. These plans can change as often as you feel necessary, but be sure to give your marketing time to work. In the end, your marketing plan should be your go-to guide for any stage of your business from opening your doors for the first time to expanding into broader markets. Your marketing strategy and plan, along with your overall business plan, takes the some of the guesswork and uncertainty out of doing business and gives you a guide to fall back on. *A marketing plan worksheet is available in the accompanying CD-ROM and in Appendix A.*

Developing Your Brand

Your brand is not just a label or logo; it is the identity of your product within your marketplace. It differentiates you from the competition, encourages repeat business, establishes a reputation, and hopefully a No. 1 preference. Consider your own shopping habits. Do you buy the same laundry detergent or shampoo every time you shop, or do you always reach for a certain brand of soda at the convenience store? This is the purchasing power of a brand name. Customers eventually buy brands automatically without considering the alternatives because they know they can expect the same experience each time they buy.

Poor products, bad customer service, or even your social reputation can affect your brand negatively. Treat your brand with care and do not ally yourself with others — including selling venues, employees, or social issues — that will offend or irritate your customers. Insist on superior product and packaging quality so customers know they can trust your product and your brand. From advertising to packaging to production practices to face-to-face exchanges, every interaction with your product affects how customers see your brand.

 TIP! Brand building begins with name recognition. Be sure your booth, your products, your clothing, your vehicle, and your signage clearly display your name and logo.

Getting started

Creating and building your brand requires you to define your goals, assess your market, examine your capabilities, and even somewhat predict the future. This process connects all the previous research you have done to the creation of your business plan and eventually to the day-to-day operations of your business. Branding goes beyond marketing because it can define how you run your business. Your ultimate goal when establishing your brand is to give customers a way to identify your product and your company quickly. One look should tell them exactly what to expect from you and your product. Here are a few suggestions to get you started on branding your product and creating a business plan:

- Identify your personal and business values. Keep it simple, but spend some time thinking about what you value and how this translates into your business. This can lead to a short slogan or a longer value statement.

- Create a mission statement. A mission statement is short, meaningful, and describes why you choose to do what you do.

- Create a vision statement. This specifies your vision for the farm and describes how you plan to achieve the goals in your mission statement. When you set targets for yourself and your business, such as getting 50 CSA subscriptions by year's end, it motivates you to work to reach those goals.

- Create a positioning statement. Positioning is your attempt to control the image of your business and represents the attribute you intend to compete on. What is the impression you hope to make in the mind of your ideal customer? You ultimately are attempting to put your brand in the top position for that sector.

Naming your farm

The name of your farm should capture its essence and tell your customers who you and what you do. Many farmers choose to use a family name for their businesses, such as Smith Farming. When you share your name and identity with your farming business, you create a personal connection with your customers and use your personal reputation or community image to build up the reputation of your farm. A plain name, though, will not really define what your farm does, so you must connect your product with that name. For example, Smith Farming could sell anything from pigs to apples. Smith's Orchards tells the customer what niche you operate in. Keep in mind that if you ever sell your business, the name will go with it, and you will not have control over how the new owner operates under your family name.

Think, too, about how you will use your name. Are you going to make T-shirts or hats? Then you will want a short name to fit this space. If possible, pick something catchy that is easy-to-say and remember, and nothing offensive or cutesy. Avoid using made-up words, acronyms, or a phrase common to your area such

as the team mascot's name. For example, if your school mascot is a Viking, your name will get lost in a sea of Vikings.

You also may want to see if the name you want is available as a website address. Even if you do not have the resources or knowledge to set up your own site right now, registering your website address or domain name is fairly inexpensive. This is a small investment for the assurance that your business name is available as a domain name when you are ready to launch a website. Check your local competition, too, so you do not choose a name similar to someone else in the marketplace, which will confuse your customers or cause them to pick your competition accidentally. Once you have chosen a name, do not alter or change it, or you will lose your brand recognition.

Legal naming issues

Before you officially name your farm, you will need to determine the legal structure of your business. The type of business you choose might affect your how your name is stated such as ending in LLC. Furthermore, you cannot use a name that you have not officially filed under. For example, you may not call yourself Smith Farming Corporation if you have not registered a corporation under that name.

Additionally, the name you want to use might already be trademarked by another business making it unavailable. Companies are quite protective of their trademarks, and if you use part or all of a trademarked name or logo, you can be hit with a "cease and desist" order, which means you must stop using this name or image in your business. If you do not cease using it, the company can sue you. Visit the United States Patent and Trademark Office (USPTO) website at **www.uspto.gov** and click on the link for Trademark Electronic Search System (TESS) to conduct a free search of registered trademarks. Other businesses in your area also might have a similar name or logo to yours and even if it is not trademarked, it is not good business etiquette to copy someone else's name. Your attorney or accountant can help you with a trademark search if needed.

Developing your logo

The logo is a visual symbol of your farm and your brand. Logos are important because they send a quick message to your consumer, leading to faster brand recognition. Your logo does not need to be dramatic, artistic, or elaborate — it can be as simple as always using the same type font or color. Whatever type of logo you choose, it should indicate something about your farm that buyers will value, such as a cow at pasture or an assortment of healthy, green veggies. Avoid using clip art available through word processing programs as these also may be used by your competition. If you or someone you know is a good artist, try drawing your own logo; just make sure it is reproducible and recognizable. If you live near a college, check with their graphic design department for a student who could help you for a reduced fee. Many do-it-yourself Web services also can walk you through creating your own logo or ask your local print shop or newspaper about their design services.

Most of the marketing areas discussed so far have mentioned that you can change as you go along — your logo is not one of those easy changes. This is something that will be with you for the long run. Consider it carefully, and do not settle for something you do not like. It is better to start without a logo and add it later, than pick one you are not sure of. Your instinct will tell you what is right, but there are a few logistical issues to consider when choosing a logo:

- **Graphically simple.** A simple graphic is easily recognizable, even from a distance, and can be enlarged or shrunken easily. This will ensure that your logo looks just as good on a small invoice as it does on a ten-foot banner.

- **Cost.** Choose a logo that also looks good in black and white. This will save you money in printing fees, as you do not need color printing for mundane items such as invoices or business cards.

- **Message.** Does your logo represent your business strategy? Is the artwork and type font consistent with the image you want to portray?

Packaging materials

Packaging speaks volumes about your product. The color and quality of packaging materials will translate into subliminal messages to your buyer but the package itself must be functional. You may have the best-looking bags, but if they are unable to hold the weight of your produce, it reflects badly on your product. If you put berries into a brown paper bag, and the acid in the berries dissolves the glue at the bottom, your customer will not be happy and likely will not purchase your products again. Investing in bags, labels, or cartons printed with your name and phone number is a great way to build your brand and garner repeat customers.

TIP! You also can appeal to customers with a "bring your own bag" strategy. When customers bring their own packaging, give them a small discount. This is not only environmentally friendly but also saves you money because you do not need packaging. Be sure to include a small thank you slip, though, with your name and logo.

Quality

You must provide quality not only in the product but also through customer service. Buyers see everything, tell their friends, and remember the next time they see you. If your produce is not good quality, either do not sell it, or mark it clearly as "seconds" and sell it at a discount for canning or preserves. Do not go to the market with substandard produce just because you did not want to miss the venue opportunity. If you or your employees are unfriendly or disorganized, customers will associate that attitude with your product. Remember, the customer is always right.

Availability and consistency

As a small farmer, you cannot guarantee that you will always have the same produce or the same quantity of produce every week. Customers expect and understand this and are usually willing to buy something similar, such as lettuce instead of spinach. Try to diversify your products enough so you will always have some-thing in the category available for sale. You also can offer a preview of coming attractions and post a list of what you plan to bring next time. If someone asks for a specific product, pay attention because this is someone you can foster into a repeat customer. You could offer to let the buyer come to the farm to pick up the item, you could deliver it when you are in the area, or offer to reserve some for them to pick up the next week.

Consistency and availability also refer to your attendance record. If you regularly go to a certain farmers' market, keep up on your attendance. Consumers depend on your product. If you are not there, they likely will go to another stall, and you might lose them as a customer.

Marketing Techniques

Marketing takes many forms from traditional printed newspaper ads to publicity stunts to good old fashioned word-of-mouth advertising. Marketing does not have to be expensive or time-consuming but it is an important expenditure in your overall budget. Do not skimp on advertising or try to cut back on your efforts as a way to save money. Your marketing efforts are the best way to reach customers effectively. This is another area where you need to think like your customer — what message will appeal to them and how can you reach them.

The business of advertising and marketing is a huge industry on its own and people who work in this field are highly trained to identify and craft the right message. To get started, you might want to consider hiring an expert to put together a marketing package for your business. This package often will include logos, small and large space ads, brochures, and event-planning ideas. Check with your local newspaper, as they often offer free advertising services if you are buying ad space. You also can use social networking sites or your local community events to get the word out, and these channels typically are free.

Traditional advertising

This method of advertising casts a wide net in hopes of finding a few customers within a broad audience. For example, one ad placed in a large metropolitan weekend newspaper will be delivered to nearly 500,000 homes. This does not mean every reader will see your ad, and those who see it might not be interested, but you will reach a large audience for a relatively low cost. Of course, many other ads will be competing for the reader's attention, which means the biggest, noisiest, splashiest ad will get the most readers. These types of ads can be expensive and not the most effective for a small business. You can, however, find small outlets with less expensive rates that will be perfectly fine for your needs.

TIP! Choose a market or selling venue that does the advertising for you, and you can piggyback on their marketing dollars.

Newspapers and print

Newspaper ads, local magazine ads, and listings in community calendars are a great way to spread the word about your current offerings or promotions. These are also the most in-expensive and the ads can be designed by the media outlet for little or no cost. You also can reproduce these ads as fliers or mini-posters and hand them out at events or hang them up on local bulletin boards. Contact your local Chamber of Commerce for information on print advertising options in your area. Tracking the success of your ads is easy, too, if you offer a coupon or other clip-type promotion. As you place your ads or fliers, put a different code on each coupon that corresponds to that placement. For instance, ads placed in the "Daily News" would have a DN in the corner of the coupon — as you get coupons at your booth you can track how many customers responded after seeing that ad.

In an effort to get the most for their money, many small business owners mistakenly load each ad with lots of information. This only results in a cluttered, confusing message. Keep your ads simple and clean — all your customer needs to know is what you are selling, what makes you different or appealing, and how to find you. More specific information can be put in other marketing materials such as brochures or websites. Be sure to stay current with your ads, and keep them fresh by changing your offer frequently.

Radio or television advertising

Radio advertising can be a good addition to your marketing plan, but you must choose stations carefully and avoid too many placements on the same station. After hearing your ad numerous times, it will just become white noise or even be annoying. Most areas have a wide variety of local stations and each serves a typical population such as country music listeners or talk radio lovers. Knowing your demographic will help you choose the station that best reaches your customer. For instance, if you are trying to reach 40-something moms, you would not want to advertise on a pop radio station during the middle of the day. The radio station can give you a chart of its demographic that clearly shows who listens and when they are tuned in.

Television advertising can be very expensive, but many stations offer an upcoming event or local spotlight segment. Check with your local stations for placement options or ideas for getting listed on their community access segments. Most broadcast ads are 30 seconds long, can be made with stock soundtracks or sound effects, and can be recorded by the station's announcers. These stations also will help you design the spot and will sometimes have the announcer read your ad live on the air.

Broadcast advertising works well in conjunction with events. For example, your radio spot could highlight an upcoming festival with: "Be sure to visit the Sunrise Farms stall at the Apple Harvest Festival held this weekend at the County Fairgrounds. They will have seven types of apples available, plus other seasonal produce, and the best homemade apple butter in the area. Mention this ad for a free apple!"

Brochures

Printed brochures are a great way to give all the details of your business and provide your customer with lots of information on your product line. Again, keep it simple, and do not cram each page with loads of type — it still needs to be readable and attractive. Most word processing programs offer a template for creating your own brochure or ask at your local print shop for services they offer.

To save money on printing, create a basic brochure about your business but do not include dates or other temporary information. You then can attach a small flier listing upcoming events without having to reprint your whole brochure. Make sure to have your brochure available at all selling venues and drop a few off at your local tourism center or chamber of commerce.

Outdoor and sign advertising

Options in outdoor signage range from huge, expensive billboards to hand-printed yard signs directing shoppers to your farm. Signage also includes the banners or signs you put in place at your selling venue. The key to good signage is readability and pertinent information. If you are directing buyers to your farm, make it readable for folks driving down the road. If you are trying to attract buyers out of a farmers' market crowd, make your banner unique and noticeable in this visually rich environment. Be sure to keep the look of your signs consistent as this will help build your brand recognition. Hiring a professional to paint your signs or create your banners is a good investment.

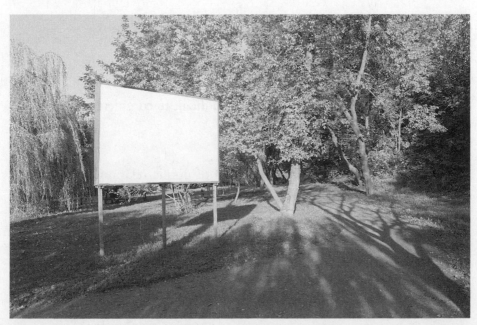

Internet

Many customers now check the Internet first when they are shopping — they especially look to the Web for unique or unusual items. Most Internet-related sales venues are free or cost a small percentage of your final sales. The best site for you depends on the products you are selling — **Etsy. com** is a great site for homemade or handmade items, **craigslist.org** and **ebay.com** are fast ways to sell produce, and **localharvest.org** gives you a place to list your farm. At the least, you can set up your own free Facebook page, which gives customers a fast way to reach you, and it costs nothing to create and run your own page.

These are all great outlets because the websites are already set up and trustworthy, the customer base is broad and active, and the payment systems are relatively low-risk. Search online by the product you are selling, and review the sites that pop up. Be sure to research their fee structures and selling policies before signing up on one of the sites. You also can look for website partners that will allow you to list your business such as your local city's website, the farmers' market site, or a community events type website.

Creating your website is an option, too, but it can be expensive and time-consuming so make sure the effort will result in more sales. Whether you use a general website or build your own, you must maintain your presence online. Online competition is cutthroat, so you must keep an active page where customers find current, easy to understand information. They will skip your page if it is too hard to maneuver or too difficult to complete an order.

Public relations

Like advertising but less direct, the goal of public relations is to create a company image through public appearances or community connections. These appearances usually are covered by the press, resulting in some publicity for your products. It might seem self-serving and a bit sneaky but you can do a lot of good for your community through your public activities — the free press is just an added bonus.

Being the news story

The story of your farm, your practices, and your product can be interesting to those living in your community and media outlets are always looking for local stories. If you have an unusual or unique product, if you are adding something to your line, or if you have a special event coming up, there will be a writer interested in telling your story. Once your photo and information appear in the paper, you basically are getting free advertising. Best of all, because it is packaged as a news story, readers do not view it as biased advertising. Send a personal note to the news desk at your local newspaper, and consider other media outlets such as regional magazines or events newspaper, health newsletters, or travel magazines.

Publicity stunts

Another way to be the news is to host an event designed to generate a buzz about your farm. Be careful to choose a stunt that is consistent with your image and showcases the factors that make your farm unique. For example, host a seasonal cook-off or taste test using your products. Make sure your name and logo are prominently displayed in a manner that will translate well into newspaper photos or television reports. Be sure the event is fun for all attendees, and hand out samples or coupons to those who come to watch. Give the press plenty of advanced warning so they can get a news crew on the scene. You also can get some free advertising before the event as the media outlets list this upcoming event. If your event is particularly successful, consider making it an annual event — people will start scheduling it into their calendars, and you will get lots of word-of-mouth advertising.

Donations

You can help your community and your business by donating products to local nonprofits or community events. Donating to these worthy causes will generate attention for your product, build your brand as an important part of the community, and give you great exposure at minimal cost. Donations made to nonprofits also may be tax deductible and are a great way to use surplus yields.

Food banks, community outreach programs, and church benefits are always looking for healthy food donations and usually list donors in their advertising or newsletters. Community festivals and events in your area almost always have food and love donations from local businesses — make sure to bring a banner or sign along displaying your name. You also can gain new customers through donations to businesses such as weight-loss clinics, day cares, culinary schools, or local gift basket raffles. This will give people a chance to try your product, which may lead them to become paying customers.

Demonstrations

Demonstrations allow people to connect a face to the product and establish you as an expert on the subject. If you are selling something unusual, showing customers how to prepare the product takes away the fear factor and lets people know they will not regret their purchase. It also gives people an opportunity to try your product and a reason to come visit your booth. Demos can be done just about anywhere and are a good option for local schools, community festivals, or on your farm. Be sure to practice safe food handling at your demo and avoid showing products that can cause allergic reactions or are too messy to eat while standing.

CASE STUDY:
COMPUTERS —
FARMER'S BEST FRIEND?

Bev Nohr
Dunlooken Farm
Glencoe, MN
dunlookenfarm@yahoo.com
320-864-5457

Dunlooken Farm is a multigenerational farm near Glencoe, Minnesota. The farm is a diverse enterprise with a CSA, dairy and meat goats, and chickens for egg production. Bev Nohr also gives riding lessons on the farm's horses. The entire family, including their three young children, pitches in to make the farm a success.

Bev has been working with horses for almost 50 years and has had goats for almost 30 years. She has also lived on a small farm almost all her life and could not remember a time when she didn't want to farm in some way. The family decided to start a CSA — which now provides most of the farm income — when they looked at Nohr's rhubarb bed and realized they had enough rhubarb for the whole county.

She considers her computer and the Internet the farm's most valuable resources. They connect her to people of a like mind, to the information she needs to make the farm a success, and to her customers. She used the Internet to conduct extensive research on her market and CSAs in general. Dunlooken Farm markets its products through an on-farm stand, CSA subscriptions, and through their e-pick option. The e-pick option allows customers to join an email list that informs customers as to which vegetables are available each week and enables them to order freshly picked vegetables that they can pick up at the farm.

Nohr stresses that the beginner wanting to start a CSA needs to learn all they can about the CSA concept, vegetable farming, and marketing. They also need to commit to a heavy workload. She says that ten-plus hour days are common during the season. She also suggests starting small and growing your business as time and your own pocketbook allows. Creativity and flexibility are a must with a CSA as sometimes things do not work, and you will have to try something new. Communication with your CSA members is also a vital skill to keep the business running smoothly and customers happy.

While Nohr handles marketing and many of the chores on the farm, she delegates organization and bookkeeping to her daughter. The best thing about farming for her is that it brings her closer to God. The worst things about farming are the heat, bugs, and the uncertainties. Traits that will make a farmer a successful include patience, imagination, a thirst for knowledge, an inborn love of farming, and stubbornness. They have found Minnesota Grown and the Minnesota Sustainable Agriculture group to be extremely helpful for their farm business with lots of resources for marketing their products.

Nohr is very optimistic about the five-year market outlook for their CSA. With the help of family, the wise use of available resources, and a lot of hard work and determination, the Dunlooken farm is thriving and has become a valuable asset to the community.

Direct marketing

While advertising and public relations get the word out to the general public, direct, personal marketing treats the customer like an individual and caters to their specific needs. By forming strong relationships with your customer base, you will build customer loyalty. This type of marketing is time-intensive so it works best in environments where the target market is clearly identified and accessible, such as a farmers' market or an organic buyers' show. Some of these methods cross over into advertising and promotion, but the key to success is to make it personal to the customer, not a broad shot to everyone in the crowd.

Direct marketing requires knowing what appeals to your customer and finding ways to meet these needs. For example, if you raise chickens, offering the chicken already cut into pieces may make your product more desirable for a customer who does not wish to tackle this part of cooking. Any face-to-face contact with a customer is basically direct marketing, but you can use a few time-tested methods to increase your business.

TIP! Always wear a "uniform" to any selling venue or public appearance. Get T-shirts, jackets, hats, or aprons printed with your name, logo, and phone number, and make sure you and your employees wear them to all events.

Repeat buyer discounts

This method targets past buyers and gives them an incentive to return. Repeat buyer discounts are no different than a membership card for a supermarket or a discount for buying in bulk. Customers are more likely to come back to you if you offer some type of discount for loyalty.

Word-of-mouth or referral incentives

A good product speaks for itself but it is even better to have your customers telling their friends. Another form of loyalty marketing, you can give your existing customers is a referral discount when they send buyers to you. For example, a CSA could offer a free month's subscription when ten of your friends sign up for a month. Obviously, you can set up your bonus however you see fit, but make sure you can handle the influx of new customers.

Event hosting

Event hosting can take many shapes for your small farm. One common example is having "pick-your-own" days or a preview sale where loyal customers get first pick of the new crop. This type of event brings customers to you, most likely will lead to large purchases, and gives your business a glow of exclusivity. You can hold a variety of events at your farm, such as a workshop on how to grow a garden or a visit from a local school or college. Whatever event you choose, just be sure it highlights your product offerings and also establishes you as the expert in your niche, be it organic farming or growing heirloom varieties.

Value-added gifts

Once you establish a loyal base, you can use incentives such as value-added gifts to increase these customers' buying habits. For example, if your customer is already buying eggs, give them a gift from another part of your farm such as jam or bread. Once they try it, they most likely will add that to their regular order. This is also a great way to build brand loyalty and get word-of-mouth advertising for your full product line. This is also a smart promotion to put in place because it allows you to use up surplus product offerings or test the market for a specific product before investing many resources in it.

Free samples

People often are stuck in their routine when it comes to grocery shopping and are hesitant to purchase new or unusual products. The last thing your customer wants is to spend money on some new product and hate it when they get home. Overcome this fear by offering free samples whenever possible, such as cut-up pieces of fruits and vegetables. If you can get a customer to sample your produce and he likes it, why would he bother going to another stall? Samples also send the message to your customers that you believe in the quality of your products.

Vineyards allow tour participants to sample different wines they produce.

Complementary partnerships

By partnering with retailers and service providers whose product offerings complement yours, you can encourage mutual sales while reaching a wider section of your target audience. For example, sell your cheese to a local winery to use for tasting events — expect to offer your cheese at a discount to the store in exchange for advertising or proceeds from in-store product sales.

Using Legal Requirements to Your Advantage

Following chapters will show you how to acquire all the necessary permits, licenses, and legal structures needed to run your business. These processes can be time-consuming and expensive, but they do provide a marketing edge to your business. Not only do they help ensure that your farm is operating within the guidelines and standards set by the government, but these licenses also send an important message to your consumer that you are serious and trustworthy.

Labeling

Your label should include information on all the licenses, certifications, or inspections you have acquired. These lend reliability to your product and will build confidence among your potential customers. Make sure your labeling is kept up-to-date as your licenses are renewed, and check with your governing agency on labeling requirements. You also can include customer-friendly information on special practices or awards such as "certified organic since 1999" or "all our animals are free-range."

Production practices

Required production practices, such as those needed for organic certification, also can be used as a marketing advantage and should be clearly stated in your advertising materials. This allows customers to see your business as a lifestyle and as a whole farm, not just as some guy with a crate of apples. For example, you could advertise that "you handpick your certified-organic berries in the morning before the dew has dried from bushes that have never been sprayed with pesticides." This gives your customer a lot of information about your farm practices, takes advantage of your certification, adds value to the product, and differentiates you from the competition. Just make sure you are not embellishing or overstating what you do.

Building and permitting

Anytime you do anything to change the landscape of your farm and a permit is required, it may be an opportunity for advertisement. Odds are that if you are building a bigger barn, it is to house more animals or more products. For example, if you build a bigger barn for the cows, you could advertise that you are expanding operations or, if the cows have more room, that your cows are the happiest because they have the biggest barn in the area. It does not need to be the center of your marketing strategy, but a small sign on your stall at the farmers' market may draw more attention.

Retailing

If you decide to go through the licensing process to retail your products directly from your farm, advertising this fact is hugely important. It tells your customers that you are proud of your farm, and you cannot wait for them to visit. Having a retail license also signals that you have high standards for your produce, and it gives your customers the assurance that your farm has passed a rigorous inspection. Distinguish yourself from the other booths at the farmers' market by letting customers know they can now come out to the farm and buy directly from you — just make sure to give out good maps with hours of operation.

Taxes

Using taxes to your advantage may sound strange, but how many times have you seen signs that a company is licensed in this state and that state? That means that they pay taxes in all of the states they are licensed in for the sales made there. As people focus more on buying local, advertising this may be an idea for some small farmers, particularly those that live near state borders. It also shows accountability, a feature that some buyers may find very attractive.

Chapter 8

Setting Up Shop: Planning, Structuring, Licensing, and Insurance

L egal issues, tax implications, and protection of assets are concerns for any new business owner You may not think farmers are subjected to lawsuits and legalities but as a small business, you are as vulnerable as any retailer — maybe even more so because you are selling food-related products. Setting up your farm as a structured business will give you the tools to weather potential legal storms, protect your assets,

and allow you to take the most profits from your business. While a business structure is important, you also must be aware of regulations, licenses, and safety standards as they apply to your products. The Small Business Administration website at

www.sba.gov has volumes of information on each of these topics, details on legal requirements, and even a chat room staffed with experts. Before you dive into setting up your business, educate yourself on all the options available to you. Take advantage of this free resource, or speak with your attorney or tax consultant for more information.

Selecting a Business Structure

There are five legally recognized types of business structures in the United States — sole proprietorships, general partnerships, cooperatives, limited liability companies (LLCs), and corporations. Each structure can be furthered refined with substructures or combined together to meet your particular needs. For example, you can set up your business as an LLC but request Subchapter S status for the corporation. Each structure brings certain tax and liability benefits but also can involve increased paperwork, expense, and operative regulations.

The legal structure you choose will form the backbone of your operation and set the platform for your everyday operations. It will influence how you proceed with financial, tax, and legal issues. It even will play a part in how you name your company, as you will be adding "Inc.," "Co.," or "LLC" at the end of the name to specify the type of company structure. Your company's legal structure also will dictate what type of documents need to be filed with the government and determine the documentation you will need to make accessible for public scrutiny. Before you officially start your farm business, you must decide which type of business structure is best for your farm, your goals, and how you plan to operate. The following sections will list, in order of difficulty and expense, the issues involved with each structure, but please check with your adviser for more information.

Sole proprietorship

Sole proprietorships are by far the easiest business structures to manage, the simplest to understand, and the least expensive to maintain. It is also the most common business structure used by small businesses. Under a sole proprietorship, you (and your spouse, if married) are the only owners and all taxes or liability protections are grouped with your personal life. You are responsible for everything — you file one income tax form and any liability coverage you have is provided under a personal insurance policy such as homeowner's insurance. Unlike most of other business types, the sole proprietorship does not need to show earnings as a company, instead all profits pass directly through to you. A sole proprietorship does not require any special paperwork — it is the de facto structure for most independent contractors or self-employed workers.

You easily can work as a sole proprietor for the rest of your career. However, without a formal business structure in place, you are personally liable for anything that goes wrong because of your business. If your product or service is faulty, if a customer falls on your property, or if your bills go unpaid, you can be sued for damages. If your business does not have enough money or assets to satisfy the lawsuit, you can be forced to use your personal money or assets to pay the bill. As mentioned earlier, proper insurance policies will cover you in many of these instances, but establishing a full separation between you and your business through a more formal structure is the only way to protect yourself completely.

If you choose to operate under a name different than your own, you must file your business under this name — also known as a fictitious name, an assumed name, a trade name, or "doing business as" (DBA.) The name chosen cannot be in use by another company and cannot pretend to be another business type such as "Smith Farms, Inc." It also must be noted that upon death of you or your spouse, a sole proprietorship automatically ends.

 FYI: Most CSAs in the United States are operated as sole proprietorships. This is not required, however, and you can choose the type of structure that works best for you.

Partnership

To form a partnership, two or more people legally agree to run a business together. Each person contributes money, property, labor, or skill and expects to share in the profits, losses, expenses, and liabilities of the business. A partnership does not pay income tax as a whole, but it must file an annual information return reporting income, deductions, gains, or losses. All profits or losses pass through to each partner who then files these amounts on individual returns.

A partnership is almost as easy to establish as a sole proprietorship, with a few exceptions. Profits and losses are shared in a partnership but not all partners necessarily have equal ownership of the business. Normally, the amount of financial or labor contributions toward the business will determine the percentage of each partner's ownership, and this is delineated in the initial partnership agreement. This percentage relates to sharing the organization's revenues as well as its financial and legal liabilities.

Although not all entrepreneurs benefit from turning their sole proprietorship into a partnership, some thrive when bringing partners into the business. Often as the business grows, the needs of the company outgrow the knowledge and capabilities of the single owner, requiring the input of someone with more knowledge or experience. Sometimes bringing on a partner can provide an influx of capital needed to expand the business. Within the confines of a partnership, you can choose to create a general partnership, a limited partnership, or a joint venture. Each of these subtypes carry unique arrangements between the partners; for example, a joint venture can be chosen to create a partnership that only lasts through the completion of a single, short-term project.

One key difference between a partnership and a sole proprietorship is that the business does not cease to exist with the death of a partner. Under such circumstances, the deceased partner's share either can be taken over by a new partner or the partnership can be reorganized to accommodate the change. In either case, the business is able to continue without much disruption.

When establishing a partnership, it is crucial to have an attorney develop the partnership agreement. These simple legal documents normally include information such as the name and purpose of the partnership, its legal address, how long the partnership is intended to last, and the names of the partners. It also addresses each partner's contribution both professionally and financially and how profits and losses will be distributed. A partnership agreement also needs to disclose how changes in the organization will be addressed, such as the death of a partner, the addition of a new partner, or the selling of one partner's interest to another individual. The agreement ultimately must address how the assets and liabilities will be distributed, should the partnership dissolve.

Limited liability company (LLC)

A limited liability company (LLC) is not quite a corporation but is much more than a partnership. An LLC has features found in the legal structure of both corporations and partnerships. It allows the owners — called members — to enjoy the liability protection of a corporation with the record-keeping flexibility of a partnership, such as not having to keep meeting minutes or records. In an LLC, the members are not personally liable for the debts incurred by the company and profits can be distributed as deemed appropriate by its members. Keep in mind the "limited" part of this title — members are not necessarily shielded from liabilities caused by wrongful acts, including those of their employees. In addition, all expenses, losses, and profits of the company flow through the business to each member, who ultimately pay either business taxes or personal taxes — but not both on the same income. Depending on the state where the LLC is formed, membership can consist of a single individual, two or more individuals, and other partnerships or corporations.

Choosing an LLC structure for your farm carries the benefit of transferring liability from you, the business owner, to the business as an entity thereby protecting your personal assets. In the same way liability remains separate between company and owner, so do the profits and assets. An LLC also carries the benefit of offering certain tax deductions that are generally only available to corporations. However, with those benefits comes an obligation to file taxes differently, which makes the LLC structure a bit more expensive and requires more paperwork. This structure is most appropriate for a business not quite large enough to warrant the expenses of incorporation or handle the responsibility of additional corporate record keeping but has operations large enough to require a better legal and financial shelter for its members. As with partnerships, the LLC can exist with various modifications but unless you are a legal whiz, these variations are best put in place with the help of an expert.

Regulations and procedures affecting the formation of LLCs differ from state to state and can be found on your secretary of state's website. There are two main documents normally filed when establishing an LLC. One is an operating agreement, which addresses issues such as the management and structure of the business, the distribution of profit and loss, the method through which members will vote, and how changes in the organizational structure will be handled. The operating agreement is not required by every state.

The second document called the "Articles of Organization" is required by every state. This form is generally available for download from your state's website. The purpose of the Articles of Organization is to establish your business legally by registering it with your state. *A sample document is included in Appendix A.* Rules do vary, but at a minimum, your document must contain the following information:

- The LLC's name and the address of the principal place of business
- The purpose of the LLC
- The name and address of the LLC's registered agent (the person who is authorized to physically accept delivery of legal documents for the company)
- The name of the manager or managing members of the company
- An effective date for the company and signatures

Cooperative

A cooperative (or co-op) is a business owned by and operated for the benefit of those using its services. Profits and earnings generated by the cooperative are used to maintain the business or returned to members, or owner-users, in the form of rebates or price reductions. Co-ops also can have non-member customers who typically pay a higher price for merchandise. A co-op usually is run by an elected board of directors and officers, but all members have voting power to control the direction of the cooperative. Members can become part of the cooperative by purchasing shares, though the amount of shares they hold does not affect the weight of their vote. This structure commonly is used in health care, art, restaurant, and agricultural industries and includes large, national chains such as the National Cooperative Grocer's Association. If you live in a rural area, you most likely are served by a co-op such as your local grain elevator or your electric company.

The process for starting a cooperative is different from other businesses because it requires a lot of advanced research and planning to identify the need, develop a strategy, and find willing members to join. While other businesses typically grow out of an individual's work or idea, a co-op aims to bring together like-minded people who already might be working in the field but separate from each other. Co-ops are not necessarily nonprofits, and they do aim to make a profit through business operations or provide a way for members to receive better pricing on goods or services. A cooperative also receives a "pass-through" designation from the IRS and does not pay federal income taxes as a business entity.

Not all cooperatives are incorporated, though many choose to do so which requires the following steps and forms:

- **Articles of Incorporation.** Among other things, you must include the name and purpose of the cooperative, the business location, duration of existence, names of the incorporators, and capital structure.

- **Conduct a charter member meeting and elect directors.** During this meeting, charter members discuss and amend proposed bylaws. By the end of the meeting, all of the charter members should vote to adopt the bylaws. If the board of directors is not already named in the articles of incorporation, you must designate them during the charter meeting.

- **Create bylaws.** Bylaws list membership requirements, duties, responsibilities and other operational procedures that allow your cooperative to run smoothly. Most states require adoption of these articles of incorporation and bylaws by a majority of your charter members.

- **Create a membership application.** To recruit members and legally verify their participation, you must issue a membership application. Membership applications include names, signatures from the board of directors, and member rights and benefits.

Depending on the type of cooperative, a variety of government-sponsored grant programs are available to co-ops. For example, the USDA Rural Development program offers grants to those establishing and operating new and existing rural development cooperatives. Some cooperatives, like credit unions and rural utility cooperatives, are exempt from all taxes due to the public-good nature of their operations. Visit the Stronger Together Co-op website at **www.strongertogether.coop** or SBA website (search for cooperative) for more information regarding the legal and tax issues related to starting and running a cooperative.

C corporation (Inc. or Ltd.)

A corporation, sometimes called a C corporation, is an independent legal entity owned collectively by those who own shares or stock in the company — called shareholders or stockholders. Shareholders can be individuals or other businesses and corporations. Decision-making is done by annual voting and day-to-day operations are done by designated employees or board members. Shareholders are not responsible for any liability including debts or lawsuits incurred by the corporation. If you choose to incorporate your farm with this structure, you essentially would become an employee of the corporation and would receive a salary, shares, or both. You are then responsible to pay personal taxes on these receipts but the corporation also pays taxes at the end of the year. Many people see this double taxation as the downside to incorporation because, as the CEO of the corporation, you pay taxes from the company's money and then pay again as an individual. Legal requirements, documentation, and shareholder contact of the corporation is also more complicated and mandated by the government and may require things like an annual meeting, electing directors, and the issuance of stock. These complexities typically make a standard C corporation burdensome for a small farm or business. The following section will discuss the subchapter S corporate form that is more applicable for a small business.

Corporations can be established as either a public or private entity. A public corporation is considered public because anyone can buy or sell stock in the company through public stock exchanges. Through their shares, stockholders have a financial interest in the company's success and often receive dividends during profitable quarters. Many corporations begin as individually owned businesses that grow to the point where selling stock is the most financially beneficial business move. However, openly trading your company's shares diminishes your control by relinquishing some of the decision-making power to shareholders and a board of directors.

A private corporation is owned and managed by a core group of shareholding decision-makers and typically involves those who started the business or those involved in the day-to-day operations of the company. Shares are held tightly within the company and are not sold on the open market. In many cases, these are family-run organizations in which family members or trusted, long-time employees are the only shareholders of the corporation. Many of America's largest, most recognized, and successful companies are privately owned including Cargill®, Publix®, Mars®, SC Johnson®, and Toys-R-Us®. These companies operate internationally, have annual revenues in the billions, and employ over 100,000 people but limit control of their company through a small collection of carefully selected private shareholders. A private corporate structure works well for a small business, too, as it allows you to stay closely involved in the operation and management of the company.

Private or public, a corporation is its own legal entity capable of entering into binding contracts and can be held directly liable in any legal issues. Its finances are not directly tied to anyone's personal finances and taxes are addressed completely separate from its owners or shareholders. Forming a corporation can be a lengthy, complicated, and expensive task and not all businesses lend themselves to this type of setup. In addition to the startup costs, there are additional ongoing maintenance costs and legal and financial reporting requirements not found in partnerships or sole proprietorships.

Forming a corporation

A corporation is formed under the laws of the state in which it is registered. To begin, you will need to establish your business name and register your legal name with your state government. If you choose to operate under a name different than the officially registered name, you must file a DBA, as discussed earlier. State laws vary, but generally corporations must include a corporate designation of corporation, incorporated, or limited at the end of the business name.

To register your business as a corporation, you need to file certain documents with your state's secretary of state office, typically Articles of Incorporation. Some states require corporations to establish directors and issue stock certificates to initial shareholders in the registration process. Contact your state business entity registration office to find out about specific filing requirements in the state where you form your business. *An example of an Article of Incorporation is included in Appendix A.*

Subchapter S corporation (or S corp.)

A variation on the corporation structure, the S-corp allows small corporations to pass corporate income, losses, deductions, and credit through to their shareholders for federal tax purposes. Consequently, the business is not taxed itself. However, any employee-shareholders must be paid reasonable compensation at fair market value, or the IRS might reclassify any additional corporate earnings as wages. This structure gives your company the benefits and protections of incorporation but preserves your tax rate as if it was a partnership, thus avoiding the double taxation problem. The S corporation was designed as a way for small businesses to incorporate themselves — in fact, this business structure can have no more than 100 shareholders.

To be considered an S corporation, you must first charter a business as a corporation in the state where it is headquartered. After you gain corporate status, all shareholders must sign an additional form (currently IRS Form 2553) to elect your corporation to become an S corporation. According to the IRS, this incorporation makes your company a unique entity, separate and apart from those who own it, and it does limit the financial liability for which you are personally responsible. Nevertheless, liability protection is limited, and you are not necessarily shielded from all litigation such as an employee's tort actions as a result of a workplace incident.

To organize as a subchapter S corporation and qualify as such under IRS regulations, the following requirements also must be met:

- All shareholders must be U.S. citizens or residents.
- All shareholders must approve operating under the S corporation legal structure.
- The corporation can only have one class of stock.

- The corporation must be able to meet the requirements for an S corporation the entire year. Form 2553, Election of Small Business Corporation, must be filed with the IRS within the first 75 days of the corporation's fiscal year.

Because of the significant role S corporations play in the U.S. economy, the S Corporation Association of America was established in 1996 and serves as a lobbying force in Washington to shield small and family-owned businesses from taxation and government mandates. Membership in the association is comprised of S corporations both big and small throughout the nation, and they keep a well-updated website with all the latest news. Visit their site at **www.s-corp.org** for more information.

Licensure

The type and scope of licenses needed for your farm depends on where you are located and the type of farm business you are operating. Federal, state, county, and local laws all have different requirements. Some market sectors are highly regulated and require special training such as the dairy industry or food service businesses. It is best to speak with your attorney to determine what is required, or recommended but optional, for your farm.

Business licenses

Business licenses regulate the existence and operation of companies. They establish location, production, and operation parameters of an individual business, such as when the business can be open. A license generally is required if you are working with animals, selling regulated items to the public such as food or liquor, or providing a service to the public that, if done incorrectly, would have grave consequences. Operating without a required license can lead to stiff fines, operational penalties, and open your business to lawsuits. Getting a license may involve training or certification, filling out an application, and paying a filing fee.

These licenses typically are issued through each state that you operate in and often on a county-by-county basis. Check with your county extension office and your secretary of state's office, or ask when you call about the sales tax permit. Most licenses need to be renewed on a regular basis, so be sure to keep track of your renewal requirements.

City business license

Many cities require an additional city-issued business license if you are operating or selling your product within their city — especially if you are selling food, liquor, or other public-health-related services. Call your city hall for information regarding what licenses and permits are needed.

When you contact the license agency, ask how long the license is good for, what the renewal process is, whether there are different levels of licensing, how much it will cost, and whether there is anything else you need to do to fulfill the law as a business within your city or county. In most cities, the city clerk does not issue business licenses but can direct you to the correct office — in some cases, you might be asked to appear before a licensing body such or the city council.

Sales tax permit

In most parts of the United States, buyers must pay a sales or consumption tax on the items they purchase. The tax is a set percentage of the total purchase price. The requirements and amounts for sales tax vary. Some places exempt food or clothing from sales tax, while others charge sales tax for prepared meals or "luxury" foods such as soda. Sales tax also can be collected at a state, county, or city level — and sometimes by all three entities. In all situations, it is the seller's responsibility to acquire the necessary permits, understand what items are taxable, collect the sales tax, and send it on to the appropriate government agency. You must pay tax on your sales whether or not you have collected it from the customer.

Check with your state's revenue office for details on the necessary sales tax collection as it relates to your product or service. Visit the website **www. sba.gov,** and look for the link to your state's revenue office. Be sure to check the rules for every state in which you sell product, as these laws often apply to where the sale is made and not where the seller lives. Sales tax also can be charged to Internet sales, and legislation is moving through many state governments to address this issue. As most laws stand now, it is the buyer's responsibility to pay sales tax for purchases made over the Internet.

Regulatory licenses

Regulatory licenses regulate actions such as production and selling practices. Contact your local health department or farm extension service to check on regulations, training, and licenses required regarding growing produce, raising animals, or handling food products. If you sell anything by weight, your scales also must be inspected.

Many farmers look at these types of inspections as wasting their time but the best approach is to welcome your inspector and encourage communication. He or she may spot something problems before they develop into big issues or may be able to advise you of upcoming changes to certain statutes. Your inspector can be an asset and is not trying to "catch you" or hurt your business.

Vehicle licenses

Depending on where you live and what type of vehicle you are driving, you might need a commercial driver's license (CDL.) The federal definition of a commercial vehicle

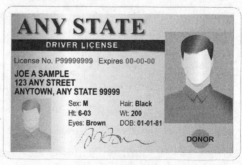

includes: "any self-propelled or towed motor vehicle used on a highway in interstate commerce with a Gross Vehicle Weight Rating (GVWR) of 26,001 pounds or more." So, a full grain trailer towed by a large tractor might qualify as needing a CDL-driver. Check with your local licensing office or visit the Department of Transportation website at **www.fmcsa.dot. gov** for more information. Laws regarding commercial vehicle traffic and licensing vary by state and might affect you if you are travelling between states — check carefully to be sure you are following all laws. At the minimum, be sure you and everyone who drives for you has up-to-date licenses without restrictions.

Organic certification

Some farmers choose to acquire optional certifications, such as being certified as organic, and this can be a great profit booster to a farm. While organic farming currently is practiced by less than 2 percent of all U.S. farmers, 28 percent of consumers buy organic products on a weekly basis. There is a huge difference, however, between all-natural and certified organic and the certification process can be lengthy, complex, and varies by type of production. For examples, land used to produce raw organic commodities must not have had prohibited substances such as pesticides applied to it for the past three years. The USDA maintains the National Organic Program and handles all certifications. They have an easy-to-use website with all the information you need to start your organic production, become certified, and market your product. Visit the site at **www.ams.usda.gov** or check at with your local USDA agent for more information.

Using Your license

After you receive your license, certification, or permit, read through the requirements, and take special care to follow all the steps listed or your license can become invalid. Considerations include:

- Renewal dates. You will be required to renew your license on a regular basis. Be sure to record this date on your calendar and submit your renewal forms a few months in advance.

- Before sending off your applications, copy all forms and supporting documents, and file these with your business records. Also, keep a copy of the approved license or permit in your files.

- Understand and follow the rules for displaying your license. Most states and localities require a prominent display where customers can see the permit.

- If you change or expand your business, your current license might not apply. Check with your licensing entity to be sure you are covered.

Insurance

Insurance is a necessary expense, and in some jurisdictions, a legal requirement for doing business. Do not assume that structuring your business as a corporation does not limit the need for the liability, asset, or employee protections offered through business insurance. No matter how careful you are, accidents will happen, and insurance is your best protection from lawsuits or loss of assets. Insurance is not a one-size-fits-all solution, and laws vary by state. Many states have minimum business insurance standards or requirements for your particular business sector. Your insurance provider also will have restrictions and can set your premiums based on your personal history, where you live, or by the risks inherent to your industry. Policies also can be written based on where you will be doing business, such as a rider for operations done at an alternate location such as a county festival.

Research each policy and provider carefully, and make sure you are comparing each policy on the same aspects. Some might have higher deductibles but lower premiums, while others might require a waiting period before claims can be made. Ask other business owners or trusted mentors for referrals to reputable insurance brokers that deal with your type of business. The most important part of this process is obtaining the proper coverage. A lower premium is not worth much if you find yourself without the insurance protection you need.

TIP! Make sure your policies are all active and in place before you start doing business. Many insurance companies have a waiting period before coverage kicks in.

You will need different types of insurance and multiple policies to cover all aspects of your business. These often can be purchased under one large umbrella policy from the same company. Many major insurance companies also offer discounts for buying more than one policy from the same agent. However, you do not have to purchase everything from the same provider and might find discounted rates if you search by individual policy.

Group buying power

As a sole proprietor or small business owner, you might find the costs of policies are much higher than you expected. In many cases, such as health insurance, premiums are kept low for large employers because large groups of people with divergent risk levels are grouped together under one policy.

When you go in to buy a single policy, you are unable to take advantage of this group buying power. Many membership groups or industry organizations, such as Farm Bureau® or your local credit union, offer group policies for this situation. Check with them or ask other small business owners for group policy recommendations.

General liability insurance

Liability insurance, also known as commercial general business liability, protects your assets by paying for costs incurred from accidents or liabilities. It covers you and your employees in all business-related activities and can be as comprehensive as paying the complete medical costs for someone injured on your farm. Liability insurance also covers the cost of your legal defense, compensatory damages, and punitive damages should you be sued successfully. General liability insurance also can protect you as a tenant if you were to cause damage to a rental property or equipment. Finally, it can cover claims of false or misleading advertising, including libel, slander, and copyright infringement. Without this coverage, you or your business will be required to pay the amount owed, even if it means liquidating assets.

General liability insurance can be purchased on its own, but it also can be included as part of a business owner's policy (BOP) which bundles liability and property insurance into one policy. If you have a BOP, make sure your liability coverage limit is sufficient to cover your needs. If it is not, you can purchase additional coverage through a separate policy. Review all your policies carefully for exclusions that might leave you vulnerable to exposure under certain circumstances. For example, if your policy excludes damage caused by drunken employees, the insurance company will not help you if an inebriated employee loses control of your farm truck.

How much liability coverage is enough?

The level of coverage you need depends on the type of business you are in and the level of risk associated with that sector. If you have a clean over-all insurance and criminal history, you will find that insurance companies price business insurance at a reasonable level so you buy a policy with a high maximum limit. Opt for the highest coverage level you can afford — you can often lower your premium by selecting a higher deductible but make sure you have enough savings put away to cover this deductible. An insurance broker who specializes in small business coverage can help you determine what you need. Do not mislead him or her — or yourself — about what you will be doing in your business, whether outlining the services you provide or the products you are offering. Ask questions, write down the coverage you need, and any promises regarding coverage from the provider or the broker, and then check these items against the actual insurance policy.

Product liability insurance

Product liability insurance is a separate category that provides protection from problems arising from the products you sell. This type of insurance would protect you if the meat you processed was contaminated and made buyers ill, for example. This type of insurance varies by state in which you sell, by the proof you have of measures or precautions taken to prevent problems, and by the relative magnitude of the risk. For example, if you make toiletries such as soap, a rash is much less serious than food poisoning.

Professional liability insurance

This type of insurance most often is used by professionals who provide an intellectually based service such as engineers, doctors, or lawyers. The purpose of this policy is to protect against malpractice, errors, or negligence in the provision of those services to your customers. This might not apply to you but check with your insurance agent to be sure.

Commercial property insurance

Different from liability this insurance covers replacement or reimbursement of property that is damaged or stolen due to fire, smoke, weather, vandalism, and so on. The definition of property includes everything from buildings to computers to loss of income — many of which might not be covered automatically under a standard homeowner's policy. This ambiguity shows why working with your insurance agent is critical in developing a policy tailored for your business.

 TIP! In some cases, you can purchase a rider to your homeowner's policy to cover business expenses. Ask your agent for details.

Crop or agricultural product insurance

The USDA's Risk Management Agency (RMA), in conjunction with private insurers, provides a wide range of agricultural-related insurance policies that cover everything from crop loss due to weather to income loss due to market fluctuation. The RMA provides policies for more than 100 crops and these policies typically include general and specific crop provisions, policy endorsements, and special circumstance provisions. The policies also have certain specifications or exclusions based on where you live. Check the "county crop program listing" at **www.rma.usda.gov** for your crop and area listing or visit with your local Farm Service Agency (FSA) agent for more information.

One policy that is particularly applicable to small farms is the Adjusted Gross Revenue-Lite or AGR-Lite program. This is a whole-farm revenue protection plan of insurance which protects against low revenue due to unavoidable natural disasters and market fluctuations. Most farm-raised crops, animals, and animal products are eligible. AGR-Lite can stand alone or be used in conjunction with other federal crop insurance plans except the standard adjusted gross revenue plan. Keep in mind, these policies often are changed, suspended, or discontinued due to federal legislation or governmental budget constraints. Stay informed by visiting the USDA site or researching it further with your extension office staff.

Vehicle insurance

Vehicle insurance is the commercial version of the insurance you already have on your private vehicle. The same price considerations apply: type of vehicle, history of claims, mileage, location, and the number and age of drivers. If you have employees who will drive your vehicles, their driving records also will be considered in the rate you pay.

Keyman insurance

Lenders who provide capital for businesses may require keyman insurance. This coverage applies to the person whose absence from the company would cause it to fail. Most likely, that person would be you or your partner. If you have borrowed money to start or operate your business, the lender may require such insurance as a guarantee of payment if anything were to happen to you.

Business interruption or criminal acts insurance

Business interruption insurance covers your expenses if you are shut down by fire, natural disaster, or other catastrophes. Criminal acts insurance protects your business against theft or malicious damage such as embezzlement or cyberattacks. The risk of these instances is low for a small business, and coverage already might be included in your general business policy. Discuss this with your provider to make sure you have adequate coverage.

Health and disability insurance

As the owner and chief operator, you are critical to your business. If you get sick or are hurt and cannot work, the company's income will suffer, which could lead to unrecoverable losses. While not true business insurance, protecting yourself with adequate health and disability insurance is important to long-range success. For example, if you were to slip and break your arm or leg, would you be able to handle your daily chores? With a disability policy in place, you would receive enough funds to cover hiring a helper until you are well enough to work again. As mentioned earlier, look into group policies offered by your church, credit union, co-op, or other like-minded groups you have membership in.

Employee-related insurance

If you choose to take on workers — full or part-time — you are required by state law to pay for certain types of insurance. This includes:

- **Workers compensation insurance.** Businesses with employees are required to carry workers' compensation insurance coverage through a commercial carrier, on a self-insured basis, or through the state workers' compensation insurance program. Visit your state's worker's compensation office or website for more information.

- **Unemployment insurance tax.** You are also required to pay unemployment insurance taxes as determined by your state. Visit the link at **www.irs.gov** to connect you with your state's agency.

- **Disability insurance.** If you are located in California, Hawaii, New Jersey, New York, Rhode Island, or Puerto Rico, disability insurance for your employees is a mandatory purchase.

Assembling a Team of Experts

Without a partner or a large in-house staff, many of these jobs will fall outside your realm of knowledge or capabilities. You also may not have enough time to run your farm efficiently while handling technical paperwork, reviewing every regulation, and staying on top of industry changes. Even if you had the time, you probably do not want to deal with these mundane aspects of running a business. Selecting a team of professionals, hired on an as-needed basis, will give you access to this knowledge when you need it. Credentialed professionals in the fields of law, banking, accounting, and insurance are a key part of a well-run business and, over time, will become trusted advisers and a crucial ingredient for your business success.

Choose people familiar with the farming industry but who are also accustomed to working with small businesses. Ask your mentors or fellow business people for referrals and be sure to include these professionals on your short list of necessary advisers:

- A certified public accountant (CPA) or someone of equal ability in accounting. You will need this person for advice and to provide services on taxes, loan negotiations, and anything to do with money. A competent accountant also can show you how to get the most profit for each dollar of income and how to organize your business to take advantage of tax laws.

- A capable business attorney. This person will help you write and review contracts, offer legal advice in hiring situations, and assist in compliance with regulations and requirements at your state and local level.

- A business-banking expert from your primary business bank. Choose a banker who is interested in the growth of your company, who can help you network with vendors, and who can assist you in finding the best investment vehicles for your business goals. Often the business banker has a deep reservoir of business knowledge that he or she would like to share with you, so ask questions. *Chapter 11 will talk about developing a banking relationship.*

- A solid business insurance agent or broker. A broker may be your wisest choice since they often compare several different policies and help you choose which is best for your situation. Remember that you might get discounts if you buy all your policies from the same agency.

As mentioned frequently throughout this book, many government programs exist to help new business owners and new farmers. The best organization for small farmers is the Small Business Administration (SBA). This agency provides free guidance to new and current business owners. The SBA can help with every part of opening and running a small business, from the business plan to weighing financing options. They have volunteers that partner with the business owner to develop the documents needed to finance the startup, to set up systems for management, and to ensure the business owner is in compliance with local, state, and federal laws.

A partner organization of the SBA, the SCORE Association (Service Corps of Retired Executives) is a nonprofit dedicated to the formation, growth, and success of small businesses nationwide. Working and retired executives and business owners donate their time and expertise and are trained as volunteer business counselors. They provide confidential counseling and mentoring, free of charge to entrepreneurs and new business owners. SCORE provides a full range of services including a thorough website with easy online mentor opportunities, local business workshops or face-to-face counseling, webinars and online workshops, and access to thousands of business experts. The SCORE website at **www.score.org** is a fabulous resource for every small business owner and makes a great complementary addition to your assembled team of experts.

Chapter 9

Business Management, Analysis, and Bookkeeping

For many business owners bookkeeping is their least favorite task. After all, you want to work the land, not push a pencil. Financial management is a necessary evil, though, and key to long-term farming success. You can hire an accountant to handle all the paperwork, but as the owner, it is important that you understand the concepts behind all the numbers. Knowing how inputs affect your bottom line, considering the factors behind risk management, and understanding employee issues all fall under your job title. An accountant can fill in the blanks but you are on the front line. Your know-how, or lack of understanding, can make the difference between profit and loss.

Creating and maintaining solid records of your financials, production costs, and expenses also gives you the ability to track a rise in expenses, to evaluate purchasing decisions, and run your business efficiently. Doing the bookkeeping yourself on a regular basis also gives you better awareness of how your whole farm is functioning. Your accountant will not recognize trends or problems until they are farther along and harder to fix.

This chapter will focus on how to develop your personal accounting system, talk about the elements that should be tracked, and offer suggestions for maximizing your profits. It also will touch on issues related to taxes and dealing with employment issues. The following sections are meant to be a primer to introduce you to the basic financial information pertinent to small business. It is recommended to do further in-depth research into each topic or consult a professional for advice.

Accounting Systems

Your accounting system begins with a simple record-keeping method to track expenditures and income. Software programs, such as QuickBooks®, make it easy to enter, sort, and compile data, and all you really need to do is enter the amounts. It is perfectly acceptable, too, to use a simple notebook or ledger sheet. Whichever system you choose, it is important to stay consistent and on top of data entry and keep good files of all receipts, invoices, and financial statements. Keeping accurate and detailed books is critically important and is the only way you can know how your business is doing and whether you are meeting projections. Your record keeping also will tell you where your marketing leads come from, how much your average customer spends, what products they prefer, what your materials cost, how much you pay your employees, and all of the other small and large details of operating a successful business.

Financially, and sometimes legally, it is necessary to establish separate bank accounts for your business. Commingling your personal funds with business resources can be confusing and risky. Start with a checking account under your business name; deposit all payments, and pay all bills from this account. If you are operating as a sole proprietorship, pay yourself a salary from the business account, and then deposit the money into your personal account. A well-documented and separate stream of money makes tax time easier and allows you to better track your business finances. Check with your accountant to be sure your records meet the reporting requirements for your chosen business structure.

As you learn more about accounting, you will need to understand a few basic terms such as:

- Cash versus accrual. The cash method involves recording a sale when the money is received and recording an expense when the cash goes out, similar to how you keep a balance in your checkbook. This type of accounting method may not give you an accurate picture of your income stream, especially if you are extending credit or going weeks before payment is received. Accrual is recording the income when you invoice the job and recording expenses when they are incurred. This means your books may show payment weeks before it actually appears in your bank account. Discuss which method is best for you with your accountant.

- Accounts receivable. Although most of your transactions will involve direct sales, you might choose to deliver product without immediate payment, such as with a wholesale customer. The amount of these outstanding but expected payments is your accounts receivable. You basically are extending credit to these customers, and the first rule of billing is to invoice customers promptly and consistently. It is equally important to send reminders, provide incentives such as discounts for early or on-time payment, or levy penalties for late payment. Most word processing and spreadsheet programs include an invoicing function.

- Double entry versus single entry. Double entry means every one of your business entries is registered twice — once as a debit, and once as a credit. You must be sure that everything balances — dollars are recorded coming in and going out. Single-entry bookkeeping is easier but is more prone to mistakes because there is no automatic balance. Your accountant probably will use the double-entry system, and most software programs will do this automatically.

- Debit versus credit. A debit is money leaving the business. A credit is money coming in to the business. For instance, if your company buys a rake, the rake's cost is a debit to you but a credit to the company who sold you the rake.

- Gross versus net. You have seen this on your personal income taxes or paycheck. Gross refers to the total monies received; net is what is left after all taxes or expenses are paid out.

- Calendar year versus fiscal year. Businesses operate on a 12-month cycle, which can begin at any time of year. If your business operates on a calendar year, that means your annual bookkeeping begins on January 1 and ends December 31. If you operate on a fiscal year, you begin your 12-month bookkeeping cycle some time after January 1 and end it 12 months from that date. Some business structures, such as sole proprietorships, are required to operate on a calendar year. Whichever way you maintain your books, your business-year structure is important for tax issues and to anchor your annual business planning and assessment.

Budgeting

Maintaining a budget is a large part of good financial management. Budgeting is essentially estimating what your future expenses and income will be. While you may not be able to say for 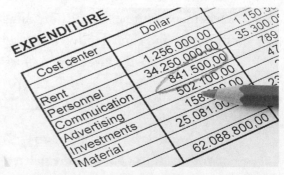 certain if your yields will be consistent or if demand will remain steady, budgeting can help you make informed plans for the future. Many farms have both a five-year budget to plan for longer-term costs such as new equipment, and current-year budget to account for operating expenses. A detailed budget will help you control your expenditures, track where your money is going, and identify how much money you will need to start your farm. Your first-year budget might just show that part of your plan is not likely to be profitable. This does not mean you should quit, but it highlights an issue you will need to address if you want to make money.

Many factors go into a budget and include operating costs, reinvestment costs, marketing costs, and emergency funds. How you gather and estimate data will greatly depend on your particular product offering and target market. For example, the first-year cost of planting fruit trees is high, and you will have to wait three years or more before you have a crop to sell. During those three years, you will not have income — unless you add another product to sell during the startup time. Knowing this information will help you assess your expected profits and shape the business so it can see net income from the start.

Quantifying your company's performance by calculating these costs also will give you a more objective view of the business and its possibilities. In the excitement of starting out, it can be too easy to inflate your perceptions of your farm's profitability and make decisions that will not pay off. By using numbers and indisputable facts, you mitigate this risk and are able to provide concrete reasons for your decisions and your ability to pay back financing. The more well-researched this section of your business plan is, the more it signals to a potential investor that you have really done your homework and have a good handle on the market at large. Most financial plans are expected to include a cash-flow forecast, a balance sheet, and an income and expense statement.

Cash-flow forecast

Cash flow is the flow of money into and out of a business. Your cash-flow forecast will help determine where income originates, how it pays your operating costs, and what you can expect to see as a profit. This forecast also will help you identify areas that can be tweaked to improve profitability.

Ideally, more money will be coming into the business than going out. Once your business has been in operation for a year or more, it will be easier to calculate expected costs.

A cash-flow forecast usually spans five years. It is really nothing more than an extended budget and includes much of the same information but is stretched out for a longer time frame. The words "forecast" and "expect" here should be red flags for you, as these projections really are only educated guesses — exact amounts of future income or expense factors cannot be anticipated, especially in farming. Keep this in mind, and do not spend your "projections" until they are in your bank. Your real takeaway from this exercise is to determine if there is a good chance that income will exceed expenditures — if not, the entire business venture needs to be reworked so it can be profitable. Most online accounting sites, basic software programs, and standard accounting books provide examples or downloadable worksheets for calculating your cash flow. *Appendix A also includes a sample worksheet.*

Balance sheet

The balance sheet is concerned with a fixed point in time and shows the immediate status and relationship of your assets to any liabilities or equity you possess. It includes accounts receivable, and all costs related to inventory, property, machinery, and supplies. Your balance sheet is not a projection or a forecast but an actual accounting of where your business stands right now. Often when taking on a partner, arranging financing, or selling your business, you will be required to provide a balance sheet for current and past years. A balance sheet how-to can be found in any accounting book, online service, or accounting software program. *Appendix A has a sample balance sheet.*

Income and expense statement

The income and expense statement, also simply referred to as the income statement, is the third and final document you need for a complete set of financials. The income statement is a projection of income and expenses for each year of business. It is basically a budget in this way but also includes noncash items, such as depreciation. An income statement breaks accounting down by variable expenses such as fuel or feed costs and fixed expenses such as property tax or interest. *An example of an income and expense statement is included in Appendix A.*

Financial Analysis

Along with preparing your financial statements, it is also necessary to perform certain types of analysis. Analyzing your expectations helps you refine your idea and gives you a framework to reference as you do business. The time might come when you want to add a new line or expand your herd; with a breakeven analysis already in place, you have the tools to determine easily if this new venture is worthwhile.

Most methods of analysis involve three basic areas that work together to determine the health of your finances:

- **Liquidity.** Liquidity refers to the ability of the farm to quickly access cash to meet immediate expenses. For example, a regular savings account is a liquid asset because you can withdraw the money on short notice while money tied up in property is less liquid because it takes time to sell the property to access the cash. Determining your level of needed liquidity can be tricky and depends on your industry and your ability to handle risk. It is necessary at least to have enough liquid assets available to meet expenses and deal with emergencies. It is also nice to have readily available cash so you can take advantage of surprises that will help your business such as getting a piece of equipment for a great price on auction.

- **Solvency.** Solvency is similar to liquidity, as it also looks at your ability to pay debts. Solvency, however, focuses on your ability to meet your long term obligations, such as your mortgage payment. It shows your ability to withstand a worst-case scenario, such as the need to liquidate assets to pay off a large debt. If you do not have enough equity or assets to meet this demand, your farm would be considered insolvent. Your accountant can help you calculate your solvency ratio.

- **Profitability.** Profitability is the measure of financial success of the farm over time. More than simply net income, profitability refers to the return you can expect on the investment you have made in the farm, as well as the ability of the farm to sustain this level of profitability. Return on investment is simply how much profit was gained or lost on an investment.

While liquidity and solvency ratios vary by industry and personal preference, your business must be profitable over time. If you are pursuing financing, you will be expected to show sufficient equity or profitability to meet your obligations. Taking on debt is not always a bad thing and can be the smart move if your business is successful. Finding the right balance of debt, though, depends on your personal preference and your long-range goals. Most financial gurus rely on breakeven and sensitivity analysis to help determine this balance. These methods assess the potential for profit, the level of risk involved, and the probability that your business will survive hard times.

Breakeven analysis

Breakeven analysis shows you the point at which revenue will cover your business expenses. Any money taken in after the breakeven point is profit. As discussed in the pricing section earlier, the breakeven strategy can be used per product to set prices, but it also helps you determine overall how much you must take in to meet expenses, fulfill long-term obligations and savings goals, and still end up with a profit.

To accurately calculate your breakeven point, you need to identify fixed and variable costs. Fixed costs, or overhead, are those costs that do not vary with production levels such as taxes, rent, or license fees. Variable costs will fluctuate according to your output and include supplies, shipping costs, fuel, and packaging. You also will need to know your average per unit selling price — this can be a general average based on your chosen prices and expected volume.

To determine your breakeven point, use this equation:
Breakeven point = fixed costs/ (unit selling price – variable costs)

This type of analysis can also show whether you can afford certain purchases, add new products, or if you can reach your desired level of income with your estimated level of production. Run a few separate calculations by treating the variant — for example, the desired income level or new purchase — as a fixed cost.

Sensitivity analysis

The sensitivity analysis looks at how sensitive your finances are to a change in variable costs, such as yield or fuel costs. When you perform a sensitivity analysis, you are calculating what the situation would be given different scenarios. For example, you may determine that if yield and crop prices are the same as last year, you will see a $30,000 profit this year. A sensitivity analysis would help also you see that in a best-case scenario of 20-percent increase in yield will net you a yearly income of $50,000.

As you know, farming is a highly unpredictable occupation, and many of these variables cannot be forecast from year to year. For this reason, it is important to calculate at least three scenarios — the best case, the worse case, and the likely case. It is nice to operate expecting the best, but if the growing season progresses and you see potential problems with yields, you can refer back to your sensitivity analysis to see how worried you should be. If this season is shaping up to be a worst case, you can shift resources and adjust practices before all is lost. This attention to possible outcomes helps you objectively analyze your business and plan ahead.

Most accounting or spreadsheet software programs offer a sensitivity analysis function. Many websites also include online calculators with which you can enter the necessary numbers. You also can ask your accountant or banking adviser to help you calculate these numbers.

Put together these financial statements and analyses also become a great planning tool from year to year. After you have accumulated a few years' data, you will spot trends in expenses or profits. You will see areas that need improvement or sectors that could be expanded. It also will be a bit of an ego boost when you see how you have progressed over the years.

Taxes

It is a fact of life in America; your business will have to pay taxes — paying the right amount of taxes depends on your bookkeeping and financial planning throughout the previous year. Tracking all expenses will make sure you take advantage of every deduction available to you. Clear, up-to-date records show the IRS that you are a responsible business owner and help avoid any suspicion of shady policies that could result in an audit. Well-filed and documented finances make the filing process quick and easy.

Depending on where you live, you might need to file and pay income and property taxes to your state, county, or city. In all cases you are required to file a federal tax return. You might also need to pay sales tax as mentioned earlier. As a business owner and farmer, your filing dates will be different than your personal return and often taxes need to be paid on a quarterly basis. Be sure to check with your accountant regarding these dates. Your local library will have all the forms you need to file your taxes, or you can find them by visiting the website **www.irs.gov**.

As your business grows, investments and expenditures can impact the amount of taxes you owe for the year. Often referred to as tax shelters, there are investment vehicles or business operating procedures that carry tax savings and benefits. This does not mean you are skirting your tax responsibility — it just means you are getting the most benefit from current tax laws. Ask your accountant and business attorney to help you understand these laws and work them into your business operating procedures and long-range planning.

Controlling Costs

Knowing all of your expenses is one thing, but keeping them under control is a whole separate endeavor. Controlling costs might prove to be the most challenging aspect of your business, but it is critically necessary to protect your profits. Many small farms, especially new ones, allow their cash flow to get out of control, and even though their accounts receivable are healthy, they do not have the money on hand to pay bills or payroll on time.

Your company's cost controls begin with finding the best price for every item you purchase, whether it is a tractor, a bag of seed, or a piece of advertising. Compare prices, look for discounts or incentives, and negotiate for a lower price. Consider buying tools or equipment second-hand or barter with a supplier to exchange goods or services. For the small farmer, the best supplier choice is often another small business — do not automatically buy everything from a big box store or continuously order from the same supplier without checking prices.

Your best price also must account for quality. Buying a poorly made tractor or low-quality seed might save you money up front but, in the end, will cost more in maintenance fees or low yield. This section will discuss ways to find savings in your costs and show areas where cheap does not equal best. The overriding factor here is to develop a frugal mindset. Learn to live with the basics because every dollar saved today will translate into profit or reinvestment monies tomorrow.

Products and materials costs

Quality supplies and materials may be expensive up front but usually end up costing less over time. The materials that go into making your final product must be top-notch, and this is not an area to be scrimped on. Whether it is topsoil, fertilizer, seeds, or packaging, stay away from the cheap, low quality. For example, questionable topsoil may be full of weed seeds that will choke your desirable plants, need additional herbicide control, or cause you to spend hours pulling weeds. In the end, these low cost inputs will result in a poor quality product and bad customer experience.

Before you try to control your costs by cutting back on production expenses, review your processes for duplicated efforts or unneeded inputs. For example, if you are spending a lot on full-color labels, then putting this in a full-color printed bag, you could save money by switching to black and white on one or both items. Streamline your process, ensure there is no waste along the production cycle, and negotiate with your vendors for the best prices. Often, you can save money through buying in bulk or through customer-loyalty programs.

Equipment purchase and maintenance

As mentioned previously, you can operate just fine with a bare bones arsenal of tools and equipment. Most of these tools can be bought at auction or second-hand and will still have a lot of years left in them. Once you have bought the equipment, it is important to keep it well maintained, even if it does cost a bit of money. Proper maintenance will extend the life of your equipment and save you money over time. Fix problems as soon as you discover them, and follow all manufacturers' recommendations regarding maintenance and parts replacement. Sometimes not following maintenance schedules can void your warranty, so review each manual carefully when you purchase the equipment. If you do not have mechanical know-how, find a trusted mechanic who can help with important maintenance. Some chores such as changing the oil or sharpening your tools is easy to learn — hire employees with mechanical abilities, ask someone to show you how to do it, or take a beginner's course at your local community college.

Keep a maintenance log for all your equipment and schedule in repairs with your other chores. Record all maintenance information including costs of parts and labor and timeline by which the maintenance is done. As equipment ages, it will begin to cost more to keep it running. When the cost of maintenance exceeds the cost of replacing the equipment, it is time to buy a replacement. Reliability is also important, and you must consider the ramifications of having a broken-down piece of equipment at a critical time in your season such as a non-working combine during harvest season. Sometimes for the health of your business, it is better to purchase new equipment that can be trusted.

Financing and banking costs

Borrowing money is nearly inevitable at some point in your business. Whether it is a long-term mortgage or a short-term line of credit, you must budget to pay loans back on time. Missing or late payments will affect your credit rating negatively, which means you will be charged higher fees and interest the next time you need to borrow money. Comparison shopping applies to banking,

too, and you should search out the lowest interest rates with the best terms. Look for checking accounts and savings accounts with no- or low-balance requirements, free check printing, and reasonable fees. These fees, closing costs, and document processing charges can raise the cost of borrowing money but vary by lender — be sure to compare each bank fairly and use the same review standards as with other vendors.

Your relationship with your banker is also important, so factor this into your research. You might be able to find a lower rate with a large online bank, but you will not receive personal service from these companies. Staying local and working with your hometown bankers also can help build your customer base and solidify your reputation in your local business economy. If you have good credit or a long-term banking relationship, most banks are willing to negotiate for your business, so do not be afraid to ask for better terms. *Chapter 11 will talk more about options in banking.*

Marketing costs

Marketing is essential to your business's well being, but it also can be a budget-buster. Before you go all out on a full-page ad, look into free or almost-free avenues of marketing. Social media, local co-op piggyback opportunities, and even hand-painted signs will get the word out without a lot of expense. Research your markets, and quiz your potential media outlets for how they reach your demographic. Avoid sales pressure to buy large, colored ads or long-term placements and opt for month-to-month placements so you can assess your efforts. As mentioned earlier, objectively look into all the ways you can advertise your business, and compare prices before committing. As your business grows, consider hiring a professional marketing company or Web designer to help build up your marketing to reach a broader audience.

Dues

Your membership in organizations such as the Chamber of Commerce, farmers' markets, or professional groups will bring you customers and valuable business connections. Membership status gives you credibility with your customers and may offer savings in materials purchases or insurance. Many organizations also will include your name and business in their printed materials, on their websites, and or even highlight your company by business category on their "recommended business" list. This is money well spent, so budget accordingly, and plan to spend several hundred dollars per year for these memberships.

Paying dues is just the first step in belonging to these groups. Membership alone does not bring in business. You must make yourself known to the group, participate in meetings, pass out business cards, work a booth at the annual fundraising picnic, and volunteer when needed. Before you spend money on memberships, make sure you have the time to follow through with an active role in the group. This time investment will pay off later in business connections, mentors, and potential customer referrals.

Employees

Hiring employees, either full- or part-time, can cost more than you anticipate. You will be responsible for taxes, worker's compensation, and possibly health and disability insurance. Having employees also entails more paperwork for taxes and legalities; more time spent interviewing, scheduling, and managing these employees; and additional expense to hire professionals to help you with paperwork. Of course, a good employee can be a real asset to your business and can grow into a trusted business partner. Additionally, having someone to share the workload takes away some of your stress and gives you more time to focus on growing the business. Employees can be hired in two separate ways: employed by your company with taxes deducted and paid in by you or hired as an independent contractor for whom you would file a 1099 income tax. Each type of employee has its pros and cons, and you can hire one or both as needed for your business. Resist the urge to pay workers "under the table" or in cash — this opens you up to potential insurance, tax, and legal problems and takes away your ability to claim this pay on your taxes.

Independent contractors

A person working as an independent contractor actually operates his or her own independent business, pays all his or her expenses, and files all payroll-related taxes — sometimes called 1099 work in reference to the tax form subcontractors file. You are not expected to pay benefits, unemployment, or other payroll taxes for this person, but you must be careful not to refer to independent contractors as "employees." The IRS is aware that businesses use contractors to avoid paying payroll taxes, so learn the current rules for 1099 work. As with anyone visiting or working on your farm, you can be held responsible for accidents or injuries that occur while the contractor is on your property.

Independent contractors, or subcontractors, often work on a project-by-project basis, and the terms of work are generally agreed upon before the job is started. For instance, you might hire an independent contractor to work in the spring to plant your fields — when the fields are fully planted, the job is over and the contractor is paid. A key difference between an independent contractor and a regular employee is that you do not have control over his or her hours or activities. You only may direct the result of the work, not the means and methods of accomplishing the result. For this reason it is important to draw up a specific, detailed contract explaining what is expected to be finished, how it will be accomplished, and the deadline for completion. If the contractor agrees to your terms but does not follow through, you will then have recourse to terminate your relationship or to not make payment.

Because they must pay their entire FICA tax, or Social Security tax, as well as their own expenses and marketing costs, independent contractors generally are paid more per hour than regular employees. Independent contractors usually work for several different clients, juggling their hours during the week to accommodate many projects at once. In most cases, subcontractors will guard your confidentiality fiercely but it is important to put a noncompete or confidentiality agreement in your contract. In addition, if you are planning to hire an independent contractor during especially high-demand times such as shearing season, get your contracts lined up early, or you might find yourself without help.

If you use an independent contractor, at tax time you will submit an IRS-approved 1099 form to the contractor, as well as a separate copy sent directly to the IRS, showing the total compensation that person received from you in the previous year. This is done, in part, to keep the contractor honest but also gives you a tax-deductible record of your business labor expenses. Independent contractors are responsible for reporting all earnings and paying all required taxes.

Full-time employees

If you hire a full-time employee, paying FICA or Social Security, workers' compensation, unemployment insurance, and, in some cases health or disability insurance expenses becomes your partial responsibility. Employers usually pay half of the necessary FICA tax, while the employee pays in the other half from his gross pay. These amounts, along with workers' compensation and other mandatory taxes, are deducted by the employer directly from the employee's paycheck. The employer then pays these monies into the appropriate government agency. Determining the amount to deduct depends on the individual employee, and this job is best hired out to a payroll service if you have numerous employees.

You also can offer job perks such as health insurance, pension benefits, or even a company vehicle. Remember that it is easier to add benefits than to take them away, so be cautious with your benefit package. You will need to offer benefits common to your industry, or you may not find workers, but you do not need to go overboard in an effort to attract employees. Your first responsibility is to your business. Research these carefully, and talk with your adviser on how best to include these items in your compensation package. The IRS employer tax information is also available in hard copy or online at the IRS website at **www.irs.gov**.

With full-time employees, you also will need to follow labor department guidelines on hiring practices, for overtime, and other employee labor rules that are not relevant to contractors. You will have more paperwork because of your employees — some states even require employers to withhold child support payments from their employee's paychecks. Consider the costs of handling this paperwork as a secondary labor expense. Having full-time employees also means you will be writing paychecks every month, even when business is slow. Be sure your expected sales can handle this burden. Ultimately, employees should create a net increase to your bottom line; do a thorough cost analysis to determine if hiring an employee still results in an adequate profit margin.

Part-time help

Managing part-time employees is much the same as full-time workers — you will still have hiring, workplace, and tax obligations, but you probably will avoid any insurance or benefit requirements. Part-time workers also can be hired or scheduled on an as-needed basis, which can be helpful during busy seasons. For many jobs on the farm, you can work with a local employment agency to find workers and that company will handle all the government paperwork. Part-timers, though, have less connection to your business and might not be as productive, skilled, or reliable as full-time workers. During especially busy times, it also might be hard to find enough part-time workers to fill all your open positions.

The definition of a part-time worker can get a bit fuzzy at times, and there really is no standard, legal definition. Some people consider part-time to be a person who is scheduled regularly to work but does not put in a full eight-hour day. Some companies consider part-time workers to be those who are "on-call" for busy times. Other businesses hire part-time workers for seasonal jobs only. In most cases, part-time employees will expect a minimum of hours every week or during the length of the season. The key is to define clearly what you mean by part-time before you start interviewing and communicate these parameters to the prospective employee. If their expectations do not meet your plans, you can be sure the employee will not stay on for long.

Chapter 10

Government Assistance to Farmers

❦

Farming is a unique industry in America because its practices and performance touch nearly every aspect of American life and well-being. A healthy farm sector bolsters the overall economy and protects our national security through a reliable and affordable food supply. Successful farmers contribute economically to local communities, state and federal tax rolls, and even in exports to other countries. Well-managed and environmentally conscious farms protect the water supply and conserve natural resources for the next generation.

Because farming plays such an important role in our overall well-being, it is highly regulated and supported through numerous federal, state, and local government programs. Many of these are in place exclusively to help farmers and provide them with training, technical assistance, and financial protections. Most of these agencies are funded through federal, state, and local taxes and are typically administered on a local basis. These farm agencies not only help with planning and education but also give out hundreds of thousands of dollars in loans, cost-shares, and grants. Many programs exist to help specifically with farm practices such as no-till farming or feedlot management. In many cases, these monies do not have to be paid back, and most loans are low cost with extremely favorable repayment terms. On a more local basis, your state, city, or county likely has special funds set up to foster new and small business development.

Funding, Loans, and Grants

Funding through government agencies takes many forms, and much of it is hidden in the resources you use everyday such as university extension websites or other governmental information websites. These ultimately are paid for through taxes but provided without charge to all citizens. The salaries paid to all extension office employees, and the resources they provide are offered at no cost to anyone who walks in the office. In many cases, these services would cost you thousands of dollars if you were receiving them through a private provider, such as a survey or engineering firm. There really is no way to quantify the costs of all the services farmers receive at no cost from the government.

Additionally, the government regularly pays out cost-share and commodity supports, and guarantees small business or farm loans through a network of private lenders, and funds grant programs. While the federal government is not as generous with its use of grants for small businesses, many state and local governments are. Some states support innovative agricultural practices through their department of agriculture while many local boards help out new or enterprising businesses. Every state has its own rules and privileges, so you will need to contact your state's economic development center or ask at your extension office for more information.

Chapter 11 and following sections will discuss monies that must be paid back, but considering grants should be your first stop for funding. Your extension office can help you locate most grants available through the USDA or other ag-related agencies. However, nearly all government departments offer grants for just about every type of project, and these may not appear in a farm-focused searched. For example, there might be Department of Education assistance available to small farmers helping young kids learn about agriculture. The best way to find information on government grants is to visit the websites at **www.grants.gov**. This site searches all federal grants and you can search by agency, by activity, by keyword, and more. The results page will direct you to the appropriate federal or state office and get you started on the application process. Make sure to plan well ahead, as it can takes months for your application to be reviews. *Application requirements and private grant sources are covered in Chapter 11.*

In general, the most assistance flows from the federal government through the USDA and its myriad departments. The agencies most applicable to small farmers will be highlighted in the beginning of the chapter. A second federal agency best suited for the small farmer is the Small Business Administration. As mentioned throughout the book, this agency offers a wide range federal aid and assistance for business owners but also maintains a thorough ag-related database. Each of these agencies have detailed, thorough, and easily searched links on their websites. They cover everything you are wondering about and some things you have not even considered. Visit each site and click through all the links. Both the USDA and SBA also have experts on staff to answer your questions. They can be reached through the hotlines or the active chat rooms at each site.

Your own state also will have an agriculture department with state-issued funds and programs along with programs funded and administered jointly with the federal government. Even more locally, you will find soil and water conservation districts (SWCD), city and county boards, or specially funded technicians and engineers to help you complete environmental- or farm-related projects. Of course, as with all government bodies, there are hoops to jump through and paperwork to fill out. Generally, these departments are interconnected and the federal, state, and local staff all work together to find you the most funding and assistance and help you through every step of the process. Use all of these sources fully; they are paid for through your taxes and are the best resource for a small farm.

This chapter will touch on the most popular governmental funding programs for farming and small business but these are just the tip of the offerings available. Not only are these diverse and interconnected agencies growing and changing, but every new farm bill also adds or takes away programs and funding. As regulations and legislation changes, so do these programs. A program to help farmers today might be eliminated in the next congressional session, or its budget may be doubled to meet a need. Again, working with these agencies' local representatives is the best way to make sure you are accessing the most appropriate program. Research each thoroughly by visiting with your extension officers, and be sure to gather information from current websites.

Federal agency: USDA or United States Department of Agriculture

Website: **usda.gov**
Information Hotline: (202) 720-2791

One of the largest government agencies, the USDA handles everything from food recalls to rural development funding to emergency disaster assistance. Numerous departments exist within the USDA to specifically help farmers, ranchers,  and alternative crop producers. If you work with land, plants, water, animals, or natural resources, there is a USDA department to help you. Even the 4-H program you and your kids are involved in is operated through a joint partnership with the USDA. In many cases, multiple programs and agencies within the USDA will apply to your situation. Your first and best stop for assistance is at your county farm office. These USDA Service Centers are located around the country and are designed as a single location where customers can access the services provided by the Farm Service Agency, Natural Resources Conservation Service, and the Rural Development agencies. Other non-USDA federal, state, county, and other governmental agency employees usually are housed in these same offices, so it is truly one-stop shopping for all your farm needs. To find the office in your area, check the yellow pages under USDA Service Center, or visit their website for the handy state and county search tool.

Before we can take a look at specific agencies, we must discuss the big, controversial elephant in the room — and that is what is commonly referred to as farm subsidies. These subsidies are provided through a complex network of USDA and other federal agencies and paid with U.S. taxpayers' dollars. This first section briefly will explain subsidies, look at the arguments for and against subsidies, and then go into the specific agencies set up within the USDA to help farmers.

Subsidies or commodity support

Originally developed in the 1930s as a financial safety net for the nation's ag producers, the federal government now administers a complex system of price supports, crop insurance, and disaster assistance — programs widely referred to as subsidies or commodity supports. The government's goal is to ensure a stable, affordable food supply by helping farmers cope with situations that negatively affect their income, such as weather variations or disaster situations, final market price drops below input costs, or other unforeseen business factors. In a nutshell, the government position is that subsidies are kept in place to protect farmers from forces outside their control. What actually constitutes a subsidy payment is a bit controversial, and people do not even agree on what should be called a subsidy. Some see all aid to farmers as a subsidy — including environmental conservation assistance, crop insurance, and even loan guarantees. Others see these aid programs and direct payments as a necessary support system to keep our food supply stable and affordable.

For decades these supports were considered untouchable government programs that would never be reduced or significantly altered. Many legislators have been elected based on their support of farm subsidies and voting against these supports was a guaranteed ticket out of office. However, the tide has turned and the farm bill is being eyed as a big-ticket program ripe for budget cuts. This shift in attitude can be attributed somewhat to the vocal opposition being raised by fiscally conservative watchdog groups and consumer advocate organizations. Some reasons for opposition commonly stated by the anti-subsidy groups include:

- Direct payments are made every year regardless of the yield or crop's profit margin. In many cases, farmers who see record yields still receive payments per bushel. Payments typically are not based on financial need but on program registration and farm practice compliance.

- Large payments are disproportionately given to big corporate farms and agribusinesses that produce only a narrow range of crops. By some estimates, 90 percent of all subsidies are paid to only five types of crop producers: corn, wheat, rice, soybeans, and cotton. Corn commodities alone exceed the billion dollar mark each year. Additionally, dairy and sugar producers have a separate price and market control system. Small farmers or those farming other commodities, such as leafy greens or fruits, qualify for very little monetary aid, especially through the direct payment or counter-cyclical payment programs.

- Nutrition advocates argue that subsidies encourage America's poor eating habits by keeping consumer prices artificially low on corn, wheat, red meat, and sugar. This, in turn, makes nutritionally poor foods such as white bread or sugary cereal less expensive than more healthful choices such as spinach or fresh fruit. Farmers who raise these alternate crops receive no subsidies, so they must sell their produce at a more expensive price.

- Even more vitriolic is the argument that subsidies are just a fancy name for "farmer welfare." Opponents do not think that one industry should be singled out for such large and far-reaching taxpayer support — especially when some farms are showing record profits. This argument has gained more strength as the economy has struggled.

- Ironically, even other government agencies criticize ag subsidies because they say subsidies encourage farmers to turn environmentally valuable grasslands or wetlands into farmland so they can start receiving payments.

The proponents of subsidies are also a strong voice and many legislators, rural economists, consumers, and farmers still believe in the power of the USDA programs. They are argue that these programs and departments are often the first and only line of defense in protecting the environment, food supply, and rural economies. In most cases, proponents agree that many of these programs could be tweaked to help the nation's economy, but they do not want them to be gutted or eliminated. The pro side points to the benefits they believe these programs have brought to farmers and America as a whole. Their argument includes:

- Because subsidies include assistance and require compliance in good farming practices, the environment at large is protected by these payments. They argue that farmers eventually return their subsidies to the public by using the money to invest in better farm practices and environmental management. Additionally, farmers who receive yearly payments plug that money back into the rural economy through equipment and supply purchases.

- General food prices have remained low and affordable, helping all families buy groceries. Without these price controls, staples such as milk, bread, and cereal would be much more expensive than they are today. Additionally, new programs within the USDA have been developed to help with all crops so alternative, healthful foods also get price support. Low-priced grain crops also help all livestock farmers because it keeps the price of feed low.

- Support of these crops and practices have helped build the ethanol and other green or alternative energy development projects. These industries are tied to a strong farm economy; without government assistance in their beginning stages, they would not have thrived. They argue that this investment eventually will move America towards energy independence.

- Small family farms across the country have been saved from bankruptcy because of the protections offered through the subsidy program. Without these supports, these farms likely would have failed, which in turn would negatively affect the economy of rural America and eventually lead to food supplies being controlled by a few large corporations.

This is a highly charged, controversial topic that has become a hot-button issue in Washington, D.C. The conversation continues to evolve and as a farmer or landowner, it is important to stay abreast of developments in this area. It is also important to make sure you are receiving all the subsidies or payment assistance you qualify for. It is, after all, funded by your tax dollars, and your competitors are likely taking advantage of every program possible. Using government assistance to its fullest advantage helps you maintain a competitive edge and gives you the support you need as you get started. You may not qualify for large subsidy payments but numerous programs are designed to help a small farmer. You will be expected to meet certain compliance standards or industry regulation, so be sure you fully understand the program. Noncompliance can lead to loss of payments or enrollment in the program. Some payments are considered income and must be reported on your taxes; be sure to check with your tax adviser.

The following sections highlight the USDA agencies best suited to help the small farmer. Each listing will show the agency's website and phone number but each of the sites can be reached through the general USDA website. From each of these links, you can order publications on individual programs, but you may be asked to pay a small printing or delivery fee. Most of these documents are available at your county extension office, officially called the USDA Service Center, and you can ask your local farm office agent to explain programs in more detail.

Farm Service Agency (FSA)

Website: **fsa.usda.gov**
Phone: check your phone book under Farm Service Agency
or USDA Service Center

Every new farmer should begin his or her plan with a visit to the local Farm Service Agency. This comprehensive agency is staffed with trained employees ready to help farmers just like you. They administer everything from farm commodity support to crop insurance to environmental technical

help and disaster assistance. The FSA's farm loan programs offer a valuable resource to establish, improve, expand, transition, and strengthen your farm or ranch. Various loan programs also are set up to help specific groups exclusively, such as beginning farmers,

those needing operational monies, women or minority farmers, rural youth, and more. The FSA maintains an office in nearly every county in the United States. Visit the FSA office early in your planning so the staff has plenty of time to enroll in the programs, funding, and technical assistance applicable to your farm

Natural Resources Conservation Service (NRCS)

Website: **nrcs.usda.gov**

Phone: Check your phone book for USDA Service Center

Formerly called the Soil Conservation Service, NRCS is a conservation leader for all natural resources, ensuring private lands are made more resilient to environmental challenges. The NRCS staff works closely with landowners through conservation planning and technical assistance designed to benefit and protect all elements of the environment. In farming, the NRCS provides technical support and funding to mitigate or fix soil erosion, enhance and improve water quality, protect wildlife habitat through conscientious farm practices, and reduce or repair damage caused by floods or other natural disasters. One primary goal of the NRCS is to work closely with farmers and landowners at a local level, and they maintain field offices in nearly every county in the nation. Many times, the NRCS staff works closely with the FSA, the SWCD, and other government agencies to develop a whole farm plan.

Start2Farm

Website: **www.start2farm.gov**

Rural Information Center Phone: (800) 633-7701

The Start2Farm site and program are a project of the National Agricultural Library in partnership with the American Farm Bureau Federation. This program is funded by the USDA with two mandates:

1. To develop a Curriculum and Training Clearinghouse for new and beginning farmers with a database made available through

the website. This database features information to help you find training, technical and legal assistance, and funding sources. The Start2Farm clearinghouse serves as a one-stop reference for anyone looking for programs and resources to start farming and to be successful in their first years as a farmer or rancher.

2. To organize a yearly national Beginning Farmers and Ranchers Conference to give young and beginning farmers an opportunity to meet and learn from ag experts and to network with other farmers from around the country. This convention usually is held in the winter months and alternates locations. Visit the website for more information.

National Agricultural Library (NAL)

Website: **nal.usda.gov**
Phone: (301) 504-5755

The National Agricultural Library is one of four national libraries and has two locations: Beltsville, Maryland, and Washington, D.C. The NAL houses one of the world's largest and most accessible agricultural information collections and serves as central point for a national network of state land-grant and U.S. Department of Agriculture field libraries. NAL's specialized information centers provide access to comprehensive and essential information resources focusing on the specific aspects of the agriculture industry including alternative farming, animal welfare, food safety, and more. In addition to general on-location reference services with interlibrary loans, the NAL maintains a vast collection of digitized resources, accessible through the Internet.

Whether you are in the beginning stages of planning your farm or know exactly what you want to do, this site is a great place to start your research. They have collected publications and links to other government agencies, universities, and private organizations and have put it all together in easily searched and readable files. You even can ask a question, and they will help with the research.

Alternative Farming Systems Information Center (AFSIC)

Website: **afsic.nal.usda.gov**
Main Office Phone: (301) 504-6559

This agency specializes in library services related to alternative agriculture practices including sustainable farm systems, crop management, and livestock raising. The AFSIC is in place to implement the NAL mission of advancing access to global agricultural information. In their broad collection, the AFSIC houses information pertaining to alternative crops, organic production, business and marketing practices, ecological pest management, minority farm issues, agritourism, and more.

The National Sustainable Agriculture Information Service (ATTRA)

Website: **attra.ncat.org**
Phone: (800) 346-9140

ATTRA is a program developed and managed by the National Center for Appropriate Technology (NCAT) and is primarily funded through a cooperative agreement with the USDA's Rural Business-Cooperative Service. Additional funding is collected through sales of ATTRA materials and from private donations. ATTRA maintains only six offices nationwide but manages an extensive website designed to collect and share a wealth of information related to sustainable farming production practices, alternative crop and livestock enterprises, and innovative marketing. Services are available to farmers, ranchers, market gardeners, extension agents, researchers, educators, farm organizations, and others involved in agriculture.

Sustainable Agriculture Research and Education Outreach (SARE)

Website: **sare.org**
Phone: (301) 405-8020

SARE Outreach is the communications and outreach arm of the Sustainable Agriculture Research and Education (SARE) Program, a USDA-funded initiative that sponsors competitive grants for sustainable agriculture research and education. SARE is dedicated to the exchange of scientific and practical information on sustainable agriculture systems. Resources include free bulletins, minimally priced CDs and  books, and a searchable database of all SARE-funded project reports. On this website you can find such recent publications and resources as: *Local Harvest: A Multi-farm CSA Handbook and Crop Rotation on Organic Farms.*

Agricultural Marketing Service (AMS)

Website: **ams.usda.gov**

The Agricultural Marketing Service covers a broad range of market needs for the farmer. These include providing standardization, grading and market news services for the five big commodity programs: dairy, fruit and vegetable, livestock and seed, poultry, and cotton and tobacco. These programs oversee marketing agreements and orders, administer research and promotion programs, and purchase commodities for federal food programs. The AMS also enforces federal laws such as the Perishable Agricultural Commodities Act and the Federal Seed Act.

For smaller industries, the AMS also administers the commodity research and promotion programs, commonly called checkoff programs. These are established under federal law at the request of their industries and derive funding through industry fees or assessments. These funds then are used to increase industry awareness through research and promotion, such as industry-specific websites or ad campaigns. These programs allow small farmers and industry stakeholders to pool their funds and develop a coordinated program of research, consumer promotion, and market development. Some small farmer industries currently being served through these programs include honey, mushrooms, blueberries, popcorn, and lamb. This program also accepts proposals for new projects from the public. Check the website for instructions on submitting your idea.

In addition, the AMS manages the National Organic Program (NOP) which establishes national production, handling, and labeling standards for organic agricultural products. The NOP also accredits the certifying agents who inspect organic production and handling operations. It runs the Transportation and Marketing Program which, among other mandates, strives to improve market access for small-to medium growers and promotes regional economic development. Many of the AMS programs also are administered in conjunction with individual state departments of agriculture.

The Farmers Market Promotion Program (FMPP)

Website: **www.ams.usda.gov/FMPP**
Phone: (202) 720-0933

This division of the AMS offers grants to help improve and expand domestic farmers' markets, roadside stands, community-supported agriculture programs (CSAs), agri-tourism activities, and other direct producer-to-consumer market opportunities. Agricultural cooperatives, producer networks, producer associations, local governments, nonprofit corporations, public benefit corporations, economic development corporations, regional farmers' market authorities, and tribal governments are among those eligible to apply. In FY2012, approximately $10 million in FMPP grants were made available — the maximum award amount per proposal is $100,000.

Risk Management Agency (RMA)

Website: **rma.usda.gov**
Phone: (202) 690-2803

The role of the RMA is to help producers manage their business risks through effective, market-based solutions. The RMA's mission is to promote, support, and regulate sound risk-management solutions to preserve and strengthen the economic stability of America's agricultural producers. As mentioned in Chapter 8, this includes managing the Federal Crop Insurance Corporation (FCIC). The RMA website has lots of actuarial information, handbooks, and bulletins pertaining to farming risks. The RMA has main offices in Washington, D.C., and in Kansas City, Missouri, but also maintains ten regional offices throughout the country. Visit the website for links and more information or ask at your local USDA Service Center.

Additional USDA offices

These are just a few of the offices within the USDA that are most helpful to the small farmer — many more narrowly focused departments function as part of this agency. The USDA system provides assistance that can help you with your individual plan. The key is to research the website and each department until you find the information best suited to your needs. As mentioned previously, check first with your FSA office because they know the department inside and out.

Federal agency: EPA or Environmental Protection Agency

Website: **epa.gov**

The U.S. Environmental Protection Agency (EPA) is another large, far-reaching governmental body affecting the lives of every American. This agency is charged with protecting the air, water, land, and people from environmental health hazards. This can include everything from air pollution to chemical spills to radon exposure. The EPA administers a wide selection of programs including the Acid Rain Hotline, Energy Star appliance program, National Poison Hotline, and more. The EPA maintains ten regional offices throughout the country and works closely with other government agencies and private entities to ensure environmental standards are met.

As a farmer, you might encounter issues on your farm such as feedlot management, pesticide use, or soil erosion that will be regulated by the EPA.

In nearly all cases, compliance will be coordinated by the FSA, SWCD, or NRCS staff member working on your project. They are knowledgeable in EPA standards and will find the correct solution or EPA staffer to remedy any problems that crop up. Nearly half of the EPA budget goes into grants to state environmental programs, nonprofits, educational institutions, and others to use for a wide variety of environmentally related projects, so, frequently, farm solutions will be funded partially by these grants. The EPA website also has a searchable database, by industry, of current regulations and compliance standards.

National Agriculture Compliance Assistance Center or Ag Center

Website: **www.epa.gov/oecaagct/agctr.html**

With support from the USDA, the EPA maintains a division called the National Agriculture Compliance Assistance Center. The Ag Center is designed to address environmental issues inherent to the agriculture industry and offers comprehensive, easy-to-understand information about approaches to compliance that are both environmentally protective and agriculturally sound. The Ag Center also supports regional and state regulatory agencies in their effort to provide compliance assistance to local agricultural communities.

Through the Ag Center website, you will find links to variety of topics including pesticide use, animal waste management, groundwater and surface water issues, pollution prevention and repair solutions, and current news on compliance and regulations. The EPA recognizes that the financial demands of a small farm create barriers to environmental compliance and is willing to help. In addition to the grants they offer, the Ag Center also offers commonsense, flexible ways to reduce the costs of meeting environmental and helps you find cost-effective ways comply with environmental regulations.

Federal agency: SBA or Small Business Administration

Website: **sba.gov**

What the USDA does for the farm side of your operation, the SBA does for the business side. However, you will have to do a bit more of the legwork as the SBA does not maintain offices in every county. The website, though, is a thorough and easily searched resource and has a search tool to access information according to your specific situation. You can find answers to every business situation on this site including licensing and permitting information, copyright and trademark tips, insurance and legal issues, and much more. In addition to an information warehouse, one of the primary functions of the SBA is to assist small business owners in securing financing. Visit the website and click on the handy "Find Loans and Grants" link — you will be directed to a search tool where you enter your specific needs. Within seconds, you will have a complete list of governmental and private co-op programs that apply to your needs with thorough information on where and how to apply for each resource.

The following chapter will explain in detail the wide range of loan guarantees made available through the SBA and discuss their partnership with commercial or nonprofit lenders. Keep in mind that the SBA does not loan money directly to small business owners, but rather provides a guarantee to the bank that you will repay your loan as promised. These are considered SBA-backed loans by the bank and often carry easier terms and more favorable loan structures than standard loans. The SBA also provides a number of non-loan financial assistance programs, such as surety bonds and venture capital search. Ongoing legislative changes may affect the operation of these programs, so be sure to check the website for more information.

State Departments of Agriculture

Every state in the nation has its own department of agriculture, and these departments are administered independently of the federal government. However, in most cases funding and program assistance comes from the

USDA and other agencies so the programs are similar in scope. Typically, your department of agriculture works with federal and local staffers to make sure all practices and products comply with both state and federal regulations. Check with your local extension office for information on your state's department or use the search tool available at **www.fsis.usda.gov**.

Cooperative Extension System and National Institute of Food and Agriculture (NIFA)

Website: **nifa.usda.gov**

The Cooperative Extension System is a nationwide, noncredit educational network with a wide range of programs to help farmers, ranchers, landowners, gardeners, and those interested in conservation. Each U.S. state and territory has a state extension office at its land-grant university along with a network of local or regional extension offices. Experts who provide useful, practical, and research-based information to agricultural producers, small business owners, youth, consumers, and others in rural areas staff these offices. A department within the USDA, NIFA is the federal partner of the Cooperative Extension System and provides federal funding to the system and, through program leadership, helps the system identify and address current issues and problems.

Public Land Grant State Universities

In 1862, the Morrill Act gave each state 30,000 acres of federal land for each member in its Congressional delegation. Most of the land then was sold by the states, and the proceeds were used to fund public colleges focusing on agriculture and the mechanical arts. These land-grant universities continue to operate today with a broader scope, and many are considered the nation's most distinguished public research universities. As part of their mission, these universities maintain a wide network of cooperative extension offices supported and funded through NIFA. The system currently includes more than 100 colleges and universities throughout the United States.

TIP! Through local colleges or community education programs, many of these universities offer reduced-cost continuing education to state residents. Check your local website, or call the admissions office for more information.

Through their extension services, many universities maintain informative websites geared to the farming situations in each state. These extension sites are very useful to the small, beginning farmer and often have staff on hand to answer your questions or direct you to resources. These folks also spend a lot of time researching issues that affect farming and work to advance the field, especially in the areas of organic or sustainable agriculture, energy use, and reducing the environmental impact of farming.

You can find just about anything farm- and food-related at these websites, and they should be a primary source for research. Of course, you do not have to use the website from your state to find good information — the topics and research extend across common farming issues. Search online by topic using the .edu ending and you will get results from numerous sources. For example, the University of Wyoming site at **uwyo.edu** has everything from mental health information for farmers experiencing a drought to tips for preserving your harvest. On the other side of the country, the University of Florida website at **ufl.edu** has it all from a guide to childproofing your farm to tips on dealing with the current oyster collapse in the Gulf. To find the land-grant extension office in your state, check at the USDA Service Center or search online under extension office. You also can click through to each extension website by following the links on the interactive U.S. map found at **www.csrees.usda.gov**.

State Departments of Natural Resources (DNR)

While two large federal departments — the Department of the Interior and the Fish and Wildlife Service — exist to protect the nation's natural resources, your state also maintains its own natural resource focused agency. Typically called the Department of Natural Resources (DNR), these state-run agencies are charged with protecting natural resources as they relate to public use of hunting, fishing, and other outdoor recreational activities. As a farmer, you will be bound by state DNR regulations if your farm practices or improvements impact a natural resource such as a lake, wetland, trout stream, or animal habitat. In nearly all cases, your extension officer or technician will work directly with the DNR to address any issues, and you will not need to do any additional paperwork. However, the cost of your project or intended farm practices might go up in response to changes required by the DNR. For example, you might need to move or improve the location of your feedlot if it is determined that runoff will go into a designated fishing area. Again, this technical assistance and funding for improvements are available through and coordinated by USDA Service Center.

State Departments of Economic Development

Every state has its own department to assist in economic development, and these agencies work closely with local governments and nonprofits to help new and established businesses start, grow, and succeed. Often, these departments partner closely with services offered through federal agencies such as the SBA. Most have searchable websites and regional offices and the typical services you can receive include:

- Startup advice, training, and resources
- Financial assistance with loans, grants, and tax-exempt bonds
- Business location and site selection assistance
- Employee recruitment and training assistance

Through the economic development department, your state tracks trends and predicts outcomes in production levels, supply and input costs, population participation, and product sales for most industries. Often in conjunction with the agriculture department, your state also will issue trend reports in consumer purchases for specific agricultural products. This can be a great research tool for a new farmer, for someone developing a new product line, or for a business looking to expand into new markets. Look on the state website for more information, or contact your city or county government to learn about local economic development services available in your area.

Local Agencies

Government assistance, regulations, and funding also exist at the local level and vary by region and industry. Your county, township, city, or regional board can set rules and regulations governing activities that are seen to affect the residents of the municipality. They also can develop special programs for funding or other financial assistance to attract or retain businesses at a local level. These programs can include assistance with promotion through regional marketing efforts, tax breaks for new businesses, or special grants based on business type. For example, in Traverse City, Michigan, the Agape Financial (**www.agapefinancialmi.org/microloans.html**) offers loans of $1000 to micro-businesses in the Grand Traverse County area. This might not seem like much money but, as part of full business plan, could be enough to help a new farmer get started.

These local agencies also may have unique regulations that apply to the issues relevant to your part of the country. For example, cold areas of the country typically put road restrictions in place in the spring when the ground thaws — this might affect your ability to move large farm machinery around when using public roads. Many areas also have industry-specific rules, such as restrictions on planting near roadways, number of animals per acre, or curbs on outdoor burner or wood stoves. Check with your county and city offices for information. Additionally, nearly all parts of the country have some form of soil and water conservation district (SWCD). These are sometimes funded and administered through state or federal offices such as the DNR or USDA. However, the SWCD, comprised of elected officials, functions independently on a local basis. The SWCD usually works closely with extension offices to complete projects or address problems.

In most cases, the people comprising these boards and offices are elected to office by local residents and often serve in office part time for no pay or for a small stipend. They could be your neighbor or fellow church member and are a great first stop if you are having problems. Often, they are willing to take your problem to a higher power or shepherd you through the process needed to get things done. Your local city hall or extension office and website will have details on how to reach the representative in your area.

The Government Network

It all seems a bit overwhelming and this chapter only briefly touched on the government agencies potentially involved in your farm business. As you probably noticed, though, it is a fairly well-organized system set up, so you do not have to call multiple agencies for one problem. The USDA Service Centers, or extension offices, are truly your one-stop shopping choice. They will connect you with the right program, the right agency, and the right funding at every level of government. All you need to do is stay on top of the paperwork and follow the compliance steps they outline for you at the beginning. These offices are not just there to help you as you start your farm; they are a service to use throughout every phase of your operation. *A handy government acronym cheat sheet is included in Appendix C.*

Chapter 11

Loans, Grants, and Investors

~~~

E ven with government funding or assistance and personal money in the bank, you most likely will need to find additional sources of financing. This does not always involve taking on more debt. Working with your banker to refinance your existing debt might help you find more money in your budget. Partnering with an investor or putting together a joint venture can provide your business with

an influx of capital and, sometimes, professional expertise. Locating private grant funding can help you build certain aspects of your business and help your community.

This chapter will walk you through the most feasible, non-governmental options available for raising capital and financing your business dreams. It will begin with the more traditional avenues of lending, then discuss the SBA loan guarantee program, and finally end with more complex types of financing such as joint ventures. Many of these options can be refined further to fit your needs and unique financing might be available based on your type of farm or product. Research your specific finance needs by talking with your local extension service, visiting the library, or online websites such as the SBA, or speaking with your tax adviser or attorney. Financing is not necessarily to be avoided and, in many cases, can be the best decision you make for your business. The key is to acquire financing that gives you proper startup money but does not add large loan payments to your operating budget.

 TIP! Visit the SBA website and look for the "Lender Toolkit." This is an up-to-date resource listing all the financing options available for small businesses with helpful links to reputable organizations in each area.

Commercial Banking

A commercial bank is likely the bank you have used since you opened your first checking account. From the local corner bank to a national chain, these banks offer a variety of services beyond lending such as checking accounts, investment vehicles such as certificates of deposit, savings accounts, and safety deposit boxes. Many commercial banks also offer credit cards and nontraditional loans, which further boost your chances of obtaining funds. Commercial banks are insured by the Federal Deposit Insurance Company (FDIC) and typically have the largest selection of institutions. Large commercial banks usually offer the most perks for business such as reduced fees, more local and national branches, and free ATM services.

This type of bank is generally your best option for securing a business or farm loan because they are more willing to work with small businesses. They are in business, too, and are looking for smart deals to boost their bottom line.

What is FDIC?

At no cost to the account holder, the Federal Deposit Insurance Corporation (FDIC) protects money deposited in United States banks. With some restrictions, the standard insurance amount is $250,000 per depositor, per insured bank, for each account ownership category. This means if your bank is robbed, if it burns down, or if it goes out of business, your money is protected by the FDIC system. Look for the FDIC sticker at your bank or visit the website at **www.fdic.gov** to learn more about this program.

Credit Unions

A credit union generally offers the same services as a commercial bank but is operated as a nonprofit. It is a cooperative-style financial institution in which members have partial ownership of the institution. Membership consists of the credit union's borrowers and depositors, and earnings are returned to members in the form of dividends or reduced interest rates. While there are exceptions, most credit unions offer higher deposit rates, lower fees, and membership perks such as group buying power. However, to get these better deals, you sometimes must pay a membership fee and keep money or accounts open and active at the credit union. In some cases, you only can join if you are already part of a group such as an alumnus/alumna or employee of a university. This members-only process allows the credit union to have lower operating costs but also results in more modest returns.

Credit unions are not all the same, and the fees, membership requirements, and available products vary widely. Some use different terminology such as "share draft account" instead of "checking account." Additionally, deposits are not insured through the FDIC. However, most national and state-chartered credit unions are insured through the National Credit Union Share

Insurance Fund (NCUSIF) with the same deposit protections as commercial banks. Comparison shopping is key when deciding between individual credit unions or when selecting a credit union over a commercial bank. Make sure you are choosing a bank with the hours, fees, rates, and service most applicable to your business needs.

Farm banks

Many banks throughout the nation are considered "farm banks" because they are defined by the Federal Reserve Board as having above-average proportions of farm real estate and production loans in their loan portfolios. These banks offer a variety of loans to farms or agribusiness firms and handle many of the loans made under the USDA's guaranteed farm loan programs. Additionally, the Farm Credit System (FCS) is a network of federally chartered borrower-owned lending institutions and related service organizations that specialize in providing credit and related services to farmers, ranchers, and producers or harvesters of aquatic products. More information about farm banks can be found at these websites:

- American Bankers Association® (ABA) (**www.aba.com**)
- Farm Credit Administration (**www.fca.gov**)
- Farm Credit System. Search by county at **www.farmcreditnetwork.com**.
- Farm Credit Council (**www.fccouncil.com**)

Building a relationship with your bank

Getting the money to finance your plan begins months or even years before you actually need it. Fostering a positive relationship with the bank staff, loan officers, and manager will help them see you as a trustworthy person and an

important part of the community. In addition, by keeping your accounts in good standing you will show that you are a competent money manager. This personal, proven relationship can make a difference in your loan approval and often will outweigh a lower credit rating or lack of collateral. Keep in mind that people do business with those they know and trust.

As a customer, you also can encourage the bank to woo you and sell you their services. This turns the tables in your favor and gives you a bit of negotiating room. Of course, you must have the numbers and credit rating to back it all up. You want the bank to be aware you are presenting them with a great opportunity, that you are serious about your business, and that you are being selective when choosing a financial ally. To aid in turning the evaluation away from you and towards the bank, try asking the banker several questions during your initial meeting, such as:

- How long has this bank been in the community, and what type of service do they practice?
- How long has your banker been with the bank, and what types of clients has he or she assisted? Does your banker have farm or small business banking experience?
- What is the bank's reputation in the business community?
- What type of criteria does the bank use for loaning to businesses?
- What is the bank's CAMEL (capital adequacy, asset quality, management, earnings, and liquidity) rating?

The CAMEL reference rating demonstrates the bank's safety and soundness rating, and they may hesitate to provide it as it is rarely given out in public. Do not let that deter you from asking. It will show that you are serious about finding a strong bank to build a good relationship and that you are well informed.

Securing the loan

Even with a close friendship, convincing a bank to loan you money and to believe in your business will require some concrete paperwork, demonstrable business acumen, and interpersonal skills. After all, you really are asking the bank to become your partner, and they must believe you are worth the risk. Be prepared to show the lender your entire business plan, all your financial statements, and maybe even a sample of your product. With the right supporting evidence and enthusiasm, you just might convince your banker to take a deeper look. Chapter 12 will show you how to write a business plan, and this will be your go-to piece when you meet with your banker. Use this plan as your documentation, put together a small presentation, and practice your sales pitch. Be sure you understand every

aspect, benefit, and potential problem of your business so you are ready with an answer. Do not be too overconfident, though, and do not downplay the known risks of starting your business. While bankers use concrete numbers to judge your creditworthiness, they also make decisions based on instinct and a willingness to take some risk.

Banks rely on some basic guidelines and lending practices to make loans, including:

- **Credit.** Banks gauge your ability to pay by your previous credit history. If you have a history of paying back your debts, they will look more favorably at giving you a loan because you have shown you are responsible with credit. You also will be judged on your ratio of credit being currently used. If all your credit cards are maxed out, you will receive an unfavorable score. As with personal loans, the bank will, in part, use your FICO score or credit rating to determine your creditworthiness. Before applying for a loan, check your score through a free reporting service such as Equifax and clean up any mistakes or issues that show up.

- **History.** If you have a history with the bank or are an established community member, the bank may feel more confident in working with you. Also, if you have a history of owning a business and can show a track record of success, they also may breathe a little easier in extending a loan to your new business venture.

- **Cosigning.** After reviewing your loan application, the bank may ask you to have a cosigner on your loan. This person or business will be responsible for paying back the loan if you do not. Think carefully before using this option because nonpayment will reflect badly on your cosigner or cause them financial hardship.

Your first stop for lending should be at the bank you use for your personal accounts. If you have accounts in good standing, they will be more inclined to help you and retain you as a customer. You also might get a better rate or a faster approval because of this relationship. Keeping all your accounts in one bank also can help your business, especially in a small community. Bankers who know you by name and character will be happy to refer you to others looking for your product or service. Of course, you must shop around a bit before committing to long-term relationships involving such large sums of money. Be sure your banker knows that you would prefer to stay with them, but you at least are checking out their competition to be sure you are getting the best bargain. You also may find that your personal bank is just not equipped to handle business- or farm-related loans. In this case, ask your banker for a referral, or check with other farmers in your area. If the bank is unable to extend you a loan, ask them to consider your loan under the SBA's guaranty program. *Information on the SBA program is covered in following sections.*

If you are having difficulty securing a large whole-farm loan, bring a smaller deal to your bank to begin with. For example, you might not find a bank willing to finance the purchase of an entire dairy operation, but you could secure financing for a piece of the business, such as a short-term loan to buy cows. Of course, you still will not be able to finance the whole by taking pieces to multiple banks. A small, short-term loan will allow the bank to test you — when you pay on time and manage the loan well, they might be more willing to finance a bigger portion.

 TIP! You may have to hear the word "no" several times before you actually understand how to get to a "yes." Do not give up; rework your presentation, gather more evidence, and keep trying.

Asset-based or collateral financing

Commercial lenders often expect borrowers to offer collateral in the form of personal or business assets, such as a home or other property. These assets then are used to secure the loan. The types of assets that are accepted as business collateral can include outstanding accounts receivable, certificates of deposit (CDs), bonds, contracts for import or export, purchase orders, existing inventory, major equipment, or franchise development. In most cases, any collateral put up against the loan will be taken if you default on the loan. Carefully consider the possible ramifications of taking this step because it means you will lose the collateral — be it your house, boat, car, or cash — if you are unable to repay the loan.

Adjustable rate mortgages (ARM) or balloon loans

These two forms of loans are attractive to small businesses because the beginning terms and rates are low and more affordable to those just starting out. They do carry risks, so it is important to research these options thoroughly before signing on. Adjustable rate mortgages (ARM) are loans with interest rates tied to the going market rate. With a standard mortgage, you pay the same interest rate ten years from now that you pay today — even if the prime rate is much lower. For example, last year you signed up for a 30-year mortgage at an interest rate of 5 percent. Today your neighbor gets the same loan at 3.5 percent. You cannot change your interest rate unless you refinance the entire loan, which can cost a lot of money in extra fees. With an ARM, the rate is tied to the prime rate and is adjusted up or down as the prime rate moves. These loans carry varying terms — such as adjustments once a year or every three years. This adjustment carries risk, though, because if the prime rate goes up significantly, so will your interest rate.

With a balloon loan, you make small payments with very little money going towards the principal amount of the loan during the first few years of your loan. At the end of the term — usually within five to ten years — you will be required to make a "balloon payment" that pays off the entire balance of the loan. If you cannot pay the balloon, the property or equipment being financed is returned to the lender. Many people who take on balloon loans agree to these terms with the expectation that business will be booming by the end of the term, and there will be plenty of money to pay off the loan. If there is not enough money to make the balloon payment, the loan sometimes can be refinanced as a standard mortgage. Consider the risks carefully of this loan structure before committing.

Small Business Administration (SBA) funding and assistance

The Small Business Administration (SBA) offers a wide range of mentorship, business development, and joint partnership opportunities to the small business owner. Highlights of the most popular programs are covered in this section and additional opportunities were covered in the previous chapter. One of the SBA's most effective small business programs is their loan guarantee program administered through a nationwide network of private and nonprofit loan providers. Through a variety of financial assistance and loan programs, the SBA helps small business owners secure financing otherwise unavailable to them due to credit problems, lack of collateral, or other personal issues. The SBA does not extend loans directly but works with a network of lending partners including traditional banks, community development organizations, and microlending institutions. The SBA guarantees repayment of these loans. So when a business applies for an SBA loan, it is actually applying for a commercial loan, structured according to SBA requirements, with an SBA guaranty.

The SBA sets strict guidelines for these loans, and you still will need to supply your bank with any paperwork they request, such as financial statements or a business plan. In many cases, SBA-guaranteed loans are not available to small businesses that have access to other financing on reasonable terms. While any participating lender can help with you SBA-backed loan, lenders who are certified or preferred can make the application process smoother and quicker. These lenders are accustomed to handling the special SBA requirements and are granted a little more leeway in the application process. It is not necessary to seek out a preferred lender, but it can make the process less stressful. What these special designations mean:

- Certified lenders. These are regular participants of the SBA programs but the SBA still double-checks the decisions of the bank before qualifying the loan.

- Preferred lenders. These lenders handle the most SBA loans and have a solid reputation with the SBA. Because of their experience, the SBA is not involved in the acceptance decision-making process. If the bank accepts the applicant, the SBA is 100 percent behind the decision.

The most popular SBA-loan programs are listed in the following sections, but many more are available according to your particular situation. Talk with your personal banker or check the SBA website for more information. Keep in mind that ongoing changes in government funding and legislation will affect the operation of these programs.

Basic 7(a) loan guaranty

The SBA's primary business loan program, the Basic 7(a) allows a maximum allowable loan of $2 million and is the SBA's most flexible business loan program in terms and eligibility requirements. It is designed to accommodate a wide variety of financing needs and most of these loans are given to meet needs such as working capital; purchases of machinery, equipment, or furniture; new construction or renovation; and debt refinancing. The guaranty level on a 7(a) loan can be up to 75 percent of the total loan made to the business if it exceeds $150,000 and 85 percent for loans less than $150,000.

The most attractive features of the 7(a) are its low down payment, comparably low interest rates, and an extended loan maturity lasting as many as ten years for working capital and 25 years for fixed assets. Prepayment of the loan may result in a small early payoff fee.

Microloan program

This short-term loan program offers small loans of up to $35,000 to small businesses starting up or growing. Funds are made available through non-profit or community-based intermediary lenders that typically require some form of collateral for the loan. The loan can be used as working capital to fund operations, to purchase inventory, supplies, or equipment, and to provide furniture and fixtures for the business.

CAPLines

A CAPLines loan is an asset-based line of credit allowing businesses to manage their short-term needs, such as to continue payroll or purchase inventory. The payback terms of a CAPLine are adjusted to fit the seasonality and cash flow of a business, such as when a business must meet operating costs while finishing a large project but will not get paid until the project is completed.

Prequalification Pilot Loan Program

This program allows a small business to have its loan application analyzed and receive a potential blessing from the SBA before a lender or institution considers it. It covers loan applications for amounts up to $250,000, and its deciding factors include credit, experience, reliability, and character. This makes it unique among many of the other loans, where the applicant must have assets in order to qualify.

The main purpose in this particular program is to help the entrepreneur strengthen his or her loan application. This program can be helpful for an applicant who has relatively good credit and a semi-established business looking to expand. The SBA will ask to see the applicant's past financial records, ratios, history, and personal credit. They then will help determine which sections of the loan request are potential red flags for the bank and recommend the most favorable terms the applicant should expect.

8(a) Business Development Program

This business assistance program is designed to provide help for small businesses that may experience challenges due to disability, minority status, or other social or economic disadvantages. The 8(a) program offers a broad scope of assistance to firms that are owned and controlled at least 51 percent by socially and economically disadvantaged individuals. These loans traditionally are used for startup or expansion business development and have helped thousands of entrepreneurs gain access to the economic mainstream or get a foothold in government contracting. Participation in the program is divided into two phases over nine years: a four-year developmental stage and a five-year transition stage.

LowDoc Program

The Low-Document, or LowDoc, Program is set up to make the application process simpler and quicker than traditional methods. It does this by reducing the size of the application form to one page for loans under $50,000. For larger loans of $50,000 to $100,000, an applicant receives the same one-page application, along with a request for his or her past three years of income tax returns. This program is one of the most popular programs offered by the SBA.

CDC/504 Program (certified development company)

The CDC/504 program is a mortgage product that supports local community developments through commercial real estate. The terms of a CDC/504 program are attractive, offering a generous 25-year fixed rate. Typically, the CDC puts up 40 percent of the amount needed, the bank puts up 50 percent, and you come up with the remaining 10 percent. Rules require that you must occupy or lease 51 percent of the building your business is located in, but you are free to lease the remaining 49 percent of the building to another business. Also, the business must create jobs within the community, and the amount of money made available is tied to the number of jobs created.

Credit Cards

Credit cards are glorified bank loans that carry high interest rates, sometimes as high as 25 percent. Unlike regular bank loans, credit card companies willingly give accounts to those with poor credit histories and often charge exorbitant maintenance fees. For the disciplined cardholder, though, credit cards can offer benefits for business money management — and in many cases, it is the only way you can do business if you deal with online or remote purchases.

Credit cards are more secure and protected than a checking account, safer than cash, and the most convenient payment method. If you buy something and it arrives broken or different than described, you can get reimbursed through the buyer's protection insurance included with most credit cards. Many cards, too, offer perks such as travel miles or dividend checks after a certain amount of purchases. You also will receive a statement every month with your purchases clearly outlined, making it easy to track spending. Establishing responsible credit card use helps build your credit rating, which can help you acquire loans from traditional channels. The key to using a credit card for business is to find a card with low fees and pay balances in full every month, so you will not be charged interest.

Online Banks and Lending Services

While most commercial banks maintain an Internet presence, some banks such as PayPal or Quicken Loans® operate exclusively online. If Internet sales are a part of your business, you most likely will need to join service such as this. PayPal is a great way to accept or send payment online and allows you to link your account to your bank or credit card without giving this information out to the person receiving the money. You will be charged a small fee to process these transactions. These online sites also offer lending and can be sources of financing for a small business owner. They usually use strict guidelines for loan amounts and payment terms, expect good credit ratings, carry application or processing fees, and will not provide personal service or room for negotiating. Online banking can have a place in your overall business but thorough research is critical to be sure you are working with a reputable company with a secure Internet address.

Peer-to-peer lending

This is a relatively new cooperative-style of micro-lending made possible through the Web. Peer-to-peer (P2P) lending connects people with money to lend to those you need to borrow it. The goal of most investors on these sites is to make money, and they can often expect a 10-percent return on their investment. However, many like to be involved because it is a truly grassroots method of helping a lot of people achieve their business dreams. The most popular websites today include **Prosper.com**® or **LendingClub. com**, and lending amounts are often quite low, sometimes in increments of $25. To secure the loan, you share your idea, define the purpose of the loan and how much you want to borrow, and then post it online. Investors will then review your proposal and hopefully offer you money to get started. Interest rates are somewhat higher than traditional banks, you will need concrete evidence to support your idea, and it may take longer to secure the loan. Each site has specific steps and guidelines for joining, so research thoroughly and carefully review any fees involved with signing up.

Crowd funding

Crowd funding brings together a group of people who pool their money and resources, usually via the Internet, to support the funding needs of others. While P2P lending typically focuses on one individual lending to another, crowd funding aims to reach a funding goal by aggregating many small investors, many of whom simply donate funds without expecting a financial return. Because of this altruistic basis, crowd funding frequently is used to fund issues-based projects such as providing money for food or schooling in third world countries.

With the JOBS Act of 2012, though, crowd funding is now allowable for small businesses and with some restrictions, businesses can now raise up to one million dollars through this source. The basic people-helping-people attitude remains with crowd funding to small businesses, though, and investors are expected to stay in it as a way to give entrepreneurs a step up. Because of this nontraditional approach, most crowd-funding opportunities do not use traditional forms of repayment or interest — some lenders even are willing to take product or service as payment. As of the writing of this book, the SEC is still working out the details, so be sure to check the SBA website for more information as you consider this source of financing.

The most recognized crowd-funding site today is the nonprofit, **Kiva.org**, and this organization works on five continents providing loans to people without access to traditional banks. As this type of lending has grown in popularity, though, many sites have emerged to help specific industries including farming. More organizations are popping up every day but a good place to start your search is with these sites current in 2012:

- **Fquare.com**: buys and leases farmland
- **Kickstarter.com**: focused on arts and entertainment
- **Rockthepost.com**: general investors for startups
- **CircleUp.com**: general small business investors

You might see some similarity between crowd funding and a CSA-type farm. Both use a community-based approach to building a business and helping others. Both, too, are rapidly evolving and definitely bear a deeper look. A great website to research crowd funding and its application to farming can be found at the University of Vermont New Farmer Project website **www.uvm.edu/newfarmer**. This site highlights specific Vermont projects currently working with this source of financing and describes how these farmers have worked through the process.

 TIP! Both P2P and crowd funding also can be a good investment once you have money to spare. Pay it forward to the next small business owner, and keep these in mind when you start considering how to spend your profits.

Family and Friend Loans or Investment

Many new farmers get their start through the benevolence of family and friends, and, often, these monies do not need to be paid back. Not only is your family willing to share their knowledge with you, but they also might be happy to loan you space in their barn, give you some land or animals, help you get your crops in, or even give you startup cash. These are all viable and perfectly acceptable sources of financing and are usually the least expensive financing alternative out there. The key to making this arrangement is to spell out — in a legal document — the terms, expectations, and plans you have for paying off the debt or sharing the profits. Working with family or friends can be quite rewarding, and the chances are that your father is happy to see you go into farming. He also is willing to help you in every way possible but making a plan up front is the best way to avoid hard feelings if things go differently than expected.

The P2P lending sites mentioned previously can be a useful way to structure loans from friends and family. Because the P2P service acts as an intermediary or broker, it can help remove any potential emotional complications from the transaction while giving the lender some reassurance that you will repay on time.

Grants

A grant is money given to another to be used for a specific purpose and typically does not have to be paid back. Grants tend to center on projects where people with money want to help people without it, and are often designed to help disadvantaged or minority groups or those working towards a common public purpose such as energy efficiency or environmental protection. In addition to the government-based grants covered in Chapter 10, many privately funded grants exist specifically to help farmers, conservationists, and small businesses. Some are even exclusively put in place to help beginning farmers or those pursuing alternative farming practices and typically originate from three sources:

- **Foundations.** These grants are from nonprofit or industry-based entities that have a philosophy or mission similar to yours. They also are willing to help you fund your endeavors in making this mission a reality. For example, if your business idea involves an eco-safe gardening practice, there may be an eco-friendly foundation that would be willing to offer you a grant. For more information on foundation grants, go to the Foundation Center's website at **www.foundationcenter.org**. Check with your trade group, too, for available grants.

- **Corporations.** Many companies set up programs in which they offer grants or will match money for the development of products and services that parallel their industry, expertise, or equipment. They also offer grants to nonprofit organizations within their community to show support for local causes. If your business idea is to establish a nonprofit organization, look around your community for existing businesses that already are involved in the type of outreach programs that align with your idea.

- **Individuals:** Generally, wealthy philanthropists set up foundations through which they issue grants. Again, it will depend on your business idea and if it strikes a chord with someone who is interested in what you are trying to accomplish, especially if your endeavor is civic-oriented. Individual grants are very competitive, and the guidelines can be highly specific in what the grant provider wants done with their money.

Finding the grant that works for you will take some research. Start by searching reputable farming websites such as **hobbyfarms.com** or websites specific to your type of farming or intended project. Ask others in your area about foundations or organizations involved in small farms — they can give you more leads to finding grants. New grants come out every year, so stay current on your research. Never pay for a grant search or send money to an application service — however, it is acceptable to hire a grant writer to complete your application. The government websites listed in Chapter 10 also have search tools to identify both government and private funds. In all cases, grants must be applied for through a Request for Proposal (RFP) that explains the criteria looked at by the organization awarding the grant. You usually can write up the grant yourself but have an attorney or other experienced grant writer review it to be sure it follows the proper form. If you are awarded grant monies, you will need to meet the conditions mandated by the grant-giver and then use the funds for the stated purpose. In many cases, you will be required to submit proof of compliance, ongoing practices, or project completion.

 TIP! Receiving a grant can make for great publicity. Alert the media, and ask your grant-giver to share the spotlight with you at a ribbon cutting or product introduction event.

Outside Investors

Beyond traditional lending, many avenues exist for outside financial support. These sources can include a partnership with a friend or stranger, a joint venture with a business person, or a remote investor who provides only capital or operating funds. In most cases of outside investments, you will be required to keep up full ownership and operation of the business but relinquish some decision-making powers. A partnership or investor relationship, though, can bring your business needed capital, expand your markets, and provide you with a knowledgeable and experienced mentor. As a small, sole proprietor, you most likely will not be ready to ally with an outside investor just yet. It does require a substantial business idea or unique product and can take a lot of legal wrangling to pull together. If you do have the next great idea, then, by all means, seek out an investor who will help you turn your small operation into a big-time venture.

The following sections briefly will describe options in outside investing. Each of these types of investors can be divided further into more complex plans — research each more thoroughly by visiting the SBA website or by speaking with your business adviser. It is essential to research each option further to understand the investing terms and responsibilities clearly; always have your attorney write up and review a contract before you commit to anything.

Simple partnership

While nothing is truly simple when it comes to business, joining forces with someone in a general partnership is the easiest way to bring capital and expertise into your business. As discussed in the business structure section, a partnership is fairly quick to put together and easy to manage. The goal is to enhance your current business by bringing someone in who can add to what you currently have. For example, you might find someone with a complementary product to expand your offerings; your new partner might bring equipment, land, or cash to build the business, or you might be able to expand into additional markets with two people working instead of one. A partnership helps you divide your workload while expanding your knowledge base and source of funding. It also gives you someone to share in decision making. The benefits are wide when partnering with another but you must be ready to share the profits and risks along with your time, resources, and business ideas. A partnership is long-term and all-in — more limited options exist in joint ventures or venture capital that will be discussed later.

Of course, there are legal documents to file and contracts to draw up. Ask your lawyer to help pull these together and assist in negotiating the terms of the partnership agreement. Typically, you each will have equal share in the company and make all decisions together. Choose a partner you enjoy being with for hours on end, make sure all parties involved understand their role in the company, how resources are allocated, and how profits are divided.

Joint ventures

Another source of outside money can be found through partnering with another business entity on a limited basis. This is not a merger or take-over; it is not a lifetime commitment, and there is no actual transfer of ownership between the two parties. The companies keep what is theirs, but combine resources in a specific common interest to create potentially more profit than what could be generated individually. Through the joint venture, each party shares assets, knowledge, market shares, or profits. You see joint ventures all around you through large retail corporations

— these agreements result is what is often called cross-promotion, product tie-ins, limited editions, or exclusive arrangements. A popular example is when McDonald's® starts offering a toy in their Happy Meals® tied in to a new movie release.

Joint ventures have two primary functions: helping a business acquire and implement new technology that will make the company function more efficiently, and enabling new markets to be opened to their product. Joint

ventures can be made between vastly different-sized businesses, such as a large consumer brands company exclusively selling a small specialty product. The small company provides the large business with a unique product offering, while the large company gives the smaller business more retail outlets and branding support. Sometimes a small business can insert itself into a larger corporation in specific markets it wants to saturate.

In a joint venture, both businesses must establish a measure of trust in order to assure the success of the venture. However, it is important to share only the essential information with each other and do not accidentally give away your business secrets or core market. As the smaller member of this venture, you will be expected to give up a portion of control over your business as a whole. With a long-range focus, though, you might be deciding whether it is more important to own 100 percent of a $1-million-dollar company or only 10 percent of a $100-million-dollar company.

The most important part of any joint venture is a well-negotiated and planned contract. As with all legal documents, make sure you take part in the initial negotiations and do not let the large company take the lead and specify the terms. Have your attorney carefully review everything before signing on. Joint venture agreements are fairly standard and straightforward agreements with a few important aspects to be covered. These include:

- How will payment be made? This can be shares of the company, a percentage of profits, or an exchange of goods and services?
- Who is responsible for making decisions and operating the business?
- How much control will you retain over the marketing and branding of your product?
- Under what terms will the joint venture dissolve?

Venture capitalist

A venture capitalist (VC) is a professional investor that invests in other businesses in the hopes of earning a large return in a short time. Venture capitalists look for companies that will command the market quickly or fill an unmet consumer need. They are different from angel investors, which will be covered in the next section. Venture capitalists are in the deal to make big money — so the stakes in such an arrangement rise compared to working with angel investors.

A venture capitalist expects to be hands-on in running the business; be prepared to share control if you look to this avenue for financial support. Partnering with these investors, though, can benefit your business by giving you access to their vast business experience and network of support. Understand, though, that a venture capitalist has only one goal and that is to get a huge return in a short amount of time. This means they might pressure you heavily and push you into expansions you might not completely agree with. You must decide if you want that type of pressure in exchange for the funding and whether you can handle having someone question your every business decision. Giving an investor too much control or a large percentage of the company means you no longer may be the main decision maker.

How to make a deal

Establishing realistic terms that work for you is the most important factor in working with a venture capitalist. Many entrepreneurs get excited over their new idea and are willing accept any amount of money on any terms to get started. Your VC will try to drive the contract process and offer terms favorable to them. Review these carefully to make sure you can meet the terms, expectations, and timelines proposed. Look at delivery expectations, company control, and the VC's level of contribution. The exit plan needs to be determined up front, too, and most VCs expect to stay with a business for five years or less. Make sure this is enough time for you to build the business into something you can still run after the VC leaves and takes their profit with them. Have your attorney review the proposal. You can change the proposed terms as you see fit — once you sign the agreement, you will be expected to meet everything on time or be considered in breach of your agreement.

A partnership with a venture capitalist can be a bit of a peculiar arrangement. On the surface you are both looking to grow the business fast and make a lot of money. Deeper down, though, you each want to walk away with the biggest share — and this is where things turn a bit adversarial. A solid, well-thought-out contract will help you enter into this partnership with no worries. If possible, keep the upper hand when looking for a VC by seeking them out after your business is up and running and showing strength in the market. You will have much better negotiating power from this position and a better chance of writing a contract favorable to you.

Angel investors

Angel investors are similar to VCs but invest in higher-risk businesses with potential for the bigger return. The term "angel" does not refer to a benefactor ready to make all of your money problems go away. More accurately, your angel is someone ready to help fund nontraditional investments that offer the greatest, but riskiest, rates of return. Angels generally have strong connections to several industries and know all the ins and outs of business negotiation, including various laws and contract negotiation. Typically they are private, wealthy investors and deal with business people who find them mostly through word-of-mouth.

Unlike traditional lenders and venture capitalists, the angel investor is willing to offer large sums of money. These sums frequently exceed the six-figure mark because the angel expects to great return on investment. They also are willing to work with startups or businesses in their infancy but expect to see a well-planned business with good prospects for profit. Many angel investors are already quite wealthy and are not necessarily looking for investments that will add to their coffers. Instead, they seek companies that will help them achieve other personal goals such as fame through a successful product line, contribution to society through medical advancement, or advancing a cause they believe in, such as environmentally conscious farming. By investing in these ventures, they can use their wealth to make a difference.

Whatever the motivation, an angel investor is not going to just hand out money because you have a good idea. They want all the same things your bank or VC wants: specific terms of operation, business and financial information, a product ready to be sold, and a personal connection to you. The one big difference from a VC contract is that the angel will give you a longer time frame to work around. They are willing to spend more time with a company before expecting any return on their investment — especially so if your company is brand-new. Angel investors will be interested in becoming a part of the business, usually as a board member, and will expect regular operational and financial updates. Every agreement is different but, in general, an angel will ask for 25 percent, which can be in the form of a cash reward or bonus, stock or ownership in the company, or possibly in trade for other goods and services. The arrangements for return usually mean the returns are made in proportion to the company's success — for example, receiving shares in a profit-making company is worth more than a one-time cash payout. Most contracts also will include rights to liquidation funds if the business fails but still has items of value to liquidate, such as equipment or inventory.

A good way to find angel investors is to research those who have succeeded in your general business sector or community at large. These people like to help out up-and-comers as long as your product does not compete with theirs. Look at your product or service, and define whom it benefits. Then, look for well-established businesses or wealthy people with an interest in that area.

Chapter 12

The Business Plan

The business plan combines everything you have learned so far with everything you want to accomplish. Official business plans tend to be feared and misunderstood by business owners, but writing everything down is the next step in making your business a reality. It is a true road map to success and will help you evaluate your present situation, visualize where you want to go, and guide you to getting there. We have put this information late in the book so you can understand all the issues that go into a business plan, but developing your plan starts with your research and never really ends. It is a changing and fluid document crucial to your company's operation and future.

The exercise of writing it out will help you flesh out your ideas and identify areas that can help or hinder your success. It will help you see potential problems and discover opportunities for making more money. Your business plan also will help you develop and express your personal business philosophy and long-term goals. This will become the framework on which you base all business decisions. Having it formally written down protects you from making emotional decisions or poorly researched course changes. Sometimes this fallback plan can make the difference when you are confronted with tough circumstances or seemingly cannot-lose business propositions.

Eventually, if you seek financing, partners, or outside investors, you will need a more official business plan. Most banks will need to see your plan as part of their vetting process, and all investors will expect to see a well-researched plan during your presentation. A business plan can include anything you think is important to your business, including references, projections, and great ideas you have for the future. It can list your mission statement, your current state of finances, and your ideas for promotion. Most business plans require documentation and descriptions relating to these areas:

- An executive summary highlighting your experience and the business' history
- A description of the business, product, or service
- Statement of business goals and plan for accomplishing these goals
- Identification of potential problems and how these will be addressed
- A marketing plan
- A business management plan and outline of organizational structure
- Future expansion or partnership goals
- Financial records including past records, capital requirements and acquisition plans, and future projections
- Supporting documentation

Most businesses review their plans every year or so to be sure things are heading in the right direction. Additionally, as your business grows, you must alter your plan to reflect changes needed to keep up with the growth. Both the SBA website and the Score website at **www.score.org** offer free, step-by-step templates for writing your business plan. These sites will explain each element of a proper business plan and walk you through putting your own plan together. A template of a generic business plan also is provided in following sections and on the accompanying CD-ROM.

The business plan is nothing more than a document that outlines your business strategy. You already have written most of the components and will only need to edit or shorten each for them to fit into the plan. While some have graphs and charts galore, others are simply text. What is most important is the ability of the document to engage the reader and for the reader to understand and believe the assumptions made. The business plan also contains certain standard elements. The actual division and headings of these elements is not as important as their inclusion in some form. They are fairly basic and may sound familiar: who, what, when, where, why, and how. The following sections will offer suggestions on what to include in your plan, but check the SBA for visual examples of successful business plans. Additionally, ask your business adviser to review your plan or help you structure it properly.

 TIP! Your word-processing program might also have a downloadable business plan template. Open a new document within the program, and check for templates.

Cover page

The cover page should be laid out with all of the information centered on the page. Write the name of your company in all capital letters in the upper half of the page. Several line spaces down, write the title "Business Plan." On the bottom half, write your company's address, your name or that of the contact person, and the current date.

Table of contents

The first page inside the plan should be the table of contents with these items listed and numbered by page. Most word processing programs will paginate your final document automatically.

Mission statement
I.   Executive summary
II. Description of proposed business
III. Management and staffing
IV. Market analysis
  a.   Industry background
  b.   Target market
  c.   Product description
V.   Marketing
  a.   Products and services
  b.   Pricing strategy
  c.   Sales/distribution plan
  d.   Advertising and promotions plan.
VI. Operations
VII. Strengths and weaknesses
VIII. Financial projections
IX. Conclusion
X.   Supporting documents

Follow this order of placement as you put your plan together — descriptions and elements of each topic are covered in the following sections.

Mission statement

After the table of contents, the first page your reader will see is a separate page displaying your mission statement. Your mission statement is highly individualized but should contain three key elements: the purpose of your business, the goods or services that you provide, and a statement of your company's attitude towards your employees and customers. It should be concise but persuasive and no longer than two paragraphs. Format it attractively on the page, and insert as a separate, beginning page in the business plan.

Executive summary

The executive summary should be one or two pages long and placed next after the mission statement. You will, however, write the executive statement last after you have written the entire business plan because it is a summary of all the information you have included in the plan. The executive statement should briefly address your intended market, the purpose of the business, where will it be located, and how it will be managed. The executive summary is meant to sum up quickly what your business is but encourage the reader to look deeper into the business plan.

Description of proposed business

Describe, in detail, the purpose of your business. State what you intend to accomplish, describe your goods and services, and discuss the role your business will play in the overall market. Explain what makes your business different from the competition. Clearly identify the goals and objectives of your business. The average length for the proposed business description section should be one or two pages.

Management and staffing

Clearly identify the owners, executive officers, management team, and planned staffing levels as they relate to the everyday operations of the business. This demonstrates that you understand the labor needs of your business, have plans to manage these adequately, and have the expertise to run the business. Describe the experience and talents levels of key employees or those you plan to hire — include yourself, if applicable. For instance, you may be the only employee now but are planning on bringing in staff with complementary experience to help expand your business. This section can be short and to the point, and you do not need to include lengthy resumes or job descriptions.

Market analysis

The market analysis section highlights the research you have done in identifying your customer, the competition, and marketplace issues relevant to your product. It also explains how you plan to meet these challenges and capitalize on marketplace issues. The results of your research and analysis covered in chapters 6 and 7 basically is condensed into a few concise pages but is one of the most comprehensive sections of the plan. It can be several pages long, depending on the number of products involved and the market you intend to cover.

Industry background

This section gives a brief description of the industry as a whole and where your product fits into this sector. You should explain gaps in the market that you can fill, competition issues that will affect your business, and any trends you have identified that will impact your product or sales. For example, the demand for organically certified produce has grown exponentially, so you are planning to expand your fruit offerings to appeal to this market.

Target market

The target market describes who you customer is and what geographic, demographic, or market factors affect this customer. Your primary target market should be narrowed done to a manageable size applicable to your product and selling venues. The reader of your business plan wants to see that you have plenty of potential customers but also that you can produce enough to meet demand.

Explain here how you gathered this data and be descriptive on the qualities of your market including possible number of prospective customers, their purchasing tendencies, and how you will use this information to reach new markets. Explain the reasons why your company will be able to compete effectively and discuss pricing or promotion strategies.

Product description

Do not just blandly describe your product or service. Share how the product was developed, why you believe in it, and what you plan to do with it in the future.

Marketing strategy

The marketing strategy element of the business plan ties closely to the market analysis and identifies how you plan to retain your current and reach new customers. The marketing strategy portion of your business plan is likely to be several pages long. For a large, well-established business, it is appropriate to prepare a separate marketing strategy plan. As a small startup, though, you can include the marketing strategy as part of the business plan.

Product information

This section highlights your product offerings as a unique player in the marketplace. What makes your product unique and different from others? What benefit will your customer get from you specifically? What kind of service will you provide to the customers to build your brand? How will you package or present your product so it will stand out from the rest?

Pricing strategy

Your pricing strategy shows that you have determined a product price that keeps you competitive but still allows a reasonable profit. Show here an explanation of how you set your prices — for example, through breakeven analysis or competitive research. Explain any special pricing offers you plan to use, such as buy-in-bulk or two-for-one promotions.

Sales and distribution

Describe the systems you will use for processing orders, working at sales venues, shipping goods, and billing your customers. Also, address what methods of payment you will accept from customers, including credit terms and discounts. Discuss the methods of distribution you anticipate using, as well as the anticipated costs associated with distribution. Identify specific sales venues such as farmers' markets or wholesalers with whom you have existing commitments.

Advertising and promotion

Discuss how you plan to advertise your products and services through market-specific channels, such as shop-local initiatives or the local foods movement. One of your goals in this section is to break down what percentage of your advertising budget will be spent in which media format. Discuss how you will track and assess your advertising efforts.

Operations

This section describes all aspects of management, manufacturing, operations, and logistic considerations of production. This includes sourcing supplies, storing inventory, managing equipment, and streamlining production. Show that you understand the process from beginning to end and explain how you will actively manage the process for efficiency. Remember that all of the information outlined in this section needs to be backed by realistic numbers, such as cost of buildings, machinery, and equipment, as well as salaries.

Discuss the business's current and proposed location, describing in detail any existing facilities or proposed purchases, such as land or animals. Include discussion of any equipment you currently have or require in order to expand.

Strengths and weaknesses

Success in the business often is determined by who can take best advantage of their strengths and of who works to overcome their weaknesses. In this section of the plan, elaborate on the particulars of your business that have allowed you or will enable you to be successful. Discuss those things that set you apart and give you an advantage over your competitors, such as your particular geographic location or a supplier you found overseas that manufactures unique products.

As hard as it may be to face weaknesses, addressing them honestly will help you overcome them. However, some weaknesses or problems in business must be dealt with to succeed such as facing environmental regulations or unpredictable weather. Showing that you understand and are prepared to handle these issues is key in this section. Every business has issues such as this and no one expects you to be different. Ignoring problems is what leads to failure. As part of an official, presentation-ready plan, keep the list of your weaknesses short. You do not want to scare off investors with worst-case scenarios. This section needs to be only one page long.

Financial projections

Financial projections normally are derived from already existing historical financial information. If you are just starting up or adding a new product, this historical financial data obviously will not be available. It is acceptable to present estimates based on similar businesses' performance or your market research. If you are using the business plan as part of the application process for a loan, be sure to match your financial projections to the loan amount being requested.

When developing your financial projections, you must consider every possible expense, expected and unexpected, yet be conservative in your forecasted revenues. Your projections should address the next three to five years, breaking down each year with the following information: forecasted income statements, cash-flow statements, balance sheets, and capital expenditure budgets. This section can take up several pages of your business plan. You might want to include some graphs in addition to the budget forms to depict the information more clearly.

Conclusion

The conclusion is the last written element of the business plan. Make use of this last opportunity to state your case wisely, highlighting key issues discussed in the plan. Wrap it up and close with a summary of your future plans for the expansion and progression of your business. Use language that will help the reader visualize what you will be able to accomplish should you receive the support you are requesting.

Supporting documents

Attaching supporting documentation to your business plan certainly will strengthen it and make it more valuable, but do not overburden it with reams of data. Before you start attaching documents, ask yourself if that particular piece of information will make a difference. If the answer is no, then leave it out. If the bank or investor reviewing your business plans wants to see a form that is not included, he or she will ask for it. Documents that you should attach include:

- Copies of the business principals' résumés
- Tax returns and personal financial statements of the principals for the last three years
- A copy of licenses, certifications, and other relevant legal documents
- A copy of the lease or purchase agreement, if you are leasing or buying land, space, or equipment
- Copies of letters of intent from suppliers

Chapter 13

Maintaining, Growing, or Selling Your Business

A s you know by now, farming is much more than a job — it is a way of life that ultimately defines who you are as a person, as a community member, and as a businessperson. It is also an unpredictable endeavor with many circumstances beyond your control. Preparing for these unknowns and positioning yourself to take advantage of opportunities will ensure the health of your farm and your business. The elements you can control can make the difference between failure and success. This chapter will focus on keeping things running smoothly and building your business into a strong competitor. It also will cover options for retirement or selling your business to new owners.

Beyond the joy of farming, most farmers aim to see regular profits over time and hopefully see the profit margin widen as the business grows. Sometimes this goal can transform into the desire to build a successful farm that can be sold or passed on to the next generation. These are all realistic goals and can be achieved by thoughtful maintenance of the business and its customers. You may have to choose between expansion and contraction, between status quo operation and bringing on a partner, or even between shutting down and starting completely over. All the tools discussed so far in starting a business factor into this maintenance and decision-making process. The good news is that running your business will get easier as you learn the ropes, gain experience in predicting outcomes, and get a feel for the general market forces.

Tracking Markets and Trends

Previous chapters have discussed market trends and how they relate to starting your business. These market forces continue to affect your business and can identify areas for growth or more profitability. Often market forces operate at opposite ends of the industry spectrum — you just need to find and solidify your position within this range. For example, one end of the organic market shrinks as people cut back on organic purchases to save money while the opposite end increases as people buy more organic produce to avoid pesticide exposure. These market-driving trends are often a result of popular culture promoting something new or media hype raising awareness. These trends can ebb and flow as consumers gather information, seek out new products, and eventually move on to the next sure thing. Individual products such as pomegranate juice or quinoa may be the rage today but on a small scale, it is difficult to identify, create, and market a trendy product before it loses popularity. You can, though, capitalize on a general trend, incorporate it into your offerings, and position yourself to take advantage of the driving market force.

Shaping your product line or business strategy to align with a trend can be a great way to weather shifting market patterns. Staying current with trends allows you to remain profitable or grow your business in line with these market changes. As a farmer-businessperson you might be happy to never change or alter your product line — and if you can stay profitable without changes, that is perfectly acceptable. However, if you want to expand your business to add a little more profit or protect your bottom line from fickle consumer purchasing, adapting to market trends is necessary to good business. Again, remember your bottom line and run the numbers before adding or subtracting a product offering. If you cannot make a profit or use this new product to bring in new customers, it might not be worth the effort or expense.

Watching the market

Tracking trends does not require highly specialized experts or technical assistance. Use the resources mentioned on the SBA and USDA websites related to trending market data. Follow your industry market publications or general small farming publications such as *Mother Earth News* or *Hobby Farm*. Keep an eye on product trends in popular media. Most important, use your most valuable market research tool: your own customer. Stay connected with your customers, and they will tell you what they are looking for.

Start with informal surveys of your customers or your social network by asking a few questions such as:

- What do you like or dislike about our product or service?
- How often do you use our product or service?
- What would cause you to use it more often?
- What do you think about our prices and delivery methods?
- Do you buy this elsewhere? If so, why?
- Would you buy X if I added it to the product line? This can include new products or expansions of existing products such as a new variety.

Make sure to reward the customers who take time to answer these questions. Add these answers to your competitive analysis, and you will have a good indication of whether or not to grow your business. If you think it is worthwhile, you also could conduct a formal market study such as those offered by market researchers or marketing firms. This will cost you money but could be worth the investment. Look in your local yellow pages for firms specializing in this type of research.

Watching your competition

Similar to watching your own market, you also must keep an eye on the competition. This will not be as easy as surveying your customers but you can gather a lot of strategic data just by looking around at your selling venues. Are vendors at the market selling the same or similar items? How does your product compare in price, quality, and presentation? Is there something missing that you could offer or is the marketplace already over-run with similar products? Conversely, is your product too different from others or are customers hesitant to try something unfamiliar?

In farming, as in any business, there is a danger of "falling in love" with your product. Just like romantic love, you stop seeing the flaws in your product but be assured your customer is not in love and will see these problems. Be critical with yourself, look at your product as it exists in the overall marketplace, and think like a customer. These reviews will lead you to a product improvement or expansion that fits into your bottom line.

Watching the economy

Economic downturns are uncontrollable and can have a significant tendency to shuffle the deck. These downturns often reveal weaknesses in business practices and planning. Successful businesses are those who able to effectively respond to change in customer demand, increased supply costs, or overall economic difficulty. This type of responsiveness includes the ability to recognize which products and services are generating the most profit, to identify what the consumer values, and to distinguish where inefficiencies lie.

Carving out a niche

A niche market is a subset of a particular market in which the producer focuses on this subset only. The niche is typically small but powerful and often has little competition. Establishing your product in its own niche can be profitable and fairly easy once you are up and running. Furthermore, niche product development is one advantage that small business has in a large market. It is much easier for a small business to fill a specific niche because it is already operating on a small scale. Big businesses often need to reduce and downsize to make niche marketing profitable.

Staying on top of market trends will help you position your farm to meet the changing demands of your consumer and possibly discover new niches. Niche marketing also does not have to be something brand new — if your particular market has an unfilled niche, you can capitalize on this by offering a product to meet that need. You then become first-to-market, which usually establishes you as the market leader and the first choice for the consumer.

As mentioned earlier, fads and trends can lead to new niches opening up in the market. Food is distinctively faddish and understanding how and why those tastes change can help you position yourself. You also can build your own mini-trend by driving demand within your selling space. Offering free samples and showing customers how to prepare or cook your product may be all it takes to start a fad. Be prepared to explain specifically why your product is better or different.

To Expand or Not to Expand

There comes a time when every business considers expansion. While this might be adding new products, creating new variations within a product line, broadening market reach, or all of the above, most successful farms must expand in some way. As time goes on, even those who are content with the present size of their business will likely encounter market saturation, shrinking customer base, increased competition, or new replacement products. To face these issues head-on, your business must examine the forces affecting change and pursue the avenues for growth. Four primary paths to expansion include: process innovation, product innovation, platform innovation, and market innovation. These are all stand-alone issues and can be pursued individually or combined to bring the most coverage to your farm business.

Process innovation

This concept deals with eliminating waste from business processes such as idle or wasted time and product waste. By concentrating on eliminating these wastes, businesses can operate more efficiently and effectively recapture time and money. An inefficient process can lead to missed selling opportunities, lost customers, lowered profit margin, and plain old stress for you. Finding ways to improve efficiency will not expand your business immediately, but it eventually will give you breathing room to add products or move into additional markets.

Sometimes increasing your bottom line can be accomplished by improving your current business practices. Take a good, hard look at how you are running your operation. Consider the little things that impact your business:

- Are you managing your time well? Do you feel overwhelmed and overworked? Maybe you need a better time management system or part-time help.

- Are your appointments and records well organized? Do you spend extra time searching for receipts? If so, you are spending time doing paperwork when you could be making money. It might be time to hire a bookkeeper.

- How are your supplier or vendor relationships? Do you continue to order from the same company? If so, are they giving you the best price?

- Where and how are you selling your product or finding new customers? Do you keep going back to the same markets but see stagnate or decreasing sales? If so, you might need to expand your selling area.

- Are you throwing away product or seeing supplies spoil before you can use them? If so, examine your ordering quantities, consider raising smaller crops, or donate products before they spoil. Donations can be good for publicity and are usually tax deductible.

- Are you using resources such as fuel, electricity, and water efficiently? Unnecessary resource use on a farm can be a budget buster. Turn off the lights, conserve water, and plan your driving routes carefully.

Think about how your business is working — or not working — and address the areas you think need fixing. Pick the easiest problem first, find the cheapest solution, and then work your way down this list.

Continuing customer service

Within the process innovation realm, customer service is key, especially in a customer-oriented business such as farming. You must maintain your existing customer base, give customers incentive to spread the word,  and seek out new markets over time. Refer to the informal customer survey mentioned previously and strive to fix each problem identified in these surveys. If you have had complaints or lost customers, address the reasons for these losses.

Increasing sales does not necessarily mean continuously seeking out new customers. Sometimes it can be as easy as nurturing the group of customers you already have. A happy customer will buy more and recommend you to their friends — and you do not have to spend any extra time or effort reaching this customer. Keep an eye on customer comments and make sure you are doing all you can to keep them happy, including:

- Fixing problems quickly and with a smile
- Thanking them for their business
- Rewarding faithful customers with added bonuses
- Helping them identify additional needs you can satisfy
- Asking them for referrals respectfully

 TIP! Remind all your employees that the customer is king. Encourage always-great customer service, good attitude, and friendly demeanor.

Product innovation

Product innovation has two components. You first can create a brand new product that is new to your business or new to the market. As a small business, be sure the product you are adding fits into your overall brand, that it can be produced at the same standard of quality, and that it appeals to your existing customer base. For example, if you already are selling tomatoes and peppers, adding onions most likely will add to sales because those stopping by to purchase tomatoes also might buy onions. Finding a good complementary product that can be produced at a profit is a great way to expand your markets without a lot of extra effort.

The second approach to product innovation is to add a variation to the products you already are producing. This can be a simple change such as a bigger size, a different delivery method, or a new flavor or variety. Again, you must innovate in such a way that your brand is protected and be sure your variation does not cannibalize your existing sales. For example, if you already offer two varieties of  squash, you probably will not gain much by adding a third variety. In most cases, your customers just will try the new variety over the old — this adds to your production costs but does not really increase sales. If you are willing to find new markets, though, over time these line expansions can build your business into a well-rounded, competitive force. Weigh your costs carefully and realistically before pursuing any product innovations.

Platform innovation

Platform innovation, although related to product innovation, is quite distinct and is more of an overall business growth strategy. Platform innovation refers to the development of an entirely new method or approach that spawns other products and provokes trends. Much like politicians, your platform directs the entire operation of your business. For example, the CSA movement grew out of a farmer's platform based on the idea that people are willing to pay more for food from local sources. By developing this idea into a functioning system, a nationwide movement was born. Creating your own or adopting an existing platform can help you move your business to the next level. In many cases, too, the platform structures are already well-thought-out, and all you need to do is plug in your business components.

Market innovation

You do not have to be tied down to one particular market for the rest of your farm life. What works today might not work tomorrow and a willingness to explore new selling opportunities is critical to moving your business forward. Chapters 6 and 7 covered researching, selecting, and reaching markets and these same lessons apply as your business grows. Take all you have learned from your customers and from your competitors, and use this knowledge to evaluate market opportunities. You might be able to add new markets such as Internet sales or a CSA while maintaining your existing markets. You also might find that you would rather shift your business into a more wholesale approach and skip the whole direct-to customer angle. Or you might want to do all three if your business can handle it. As always, keeping an eye on the profit margin will help you make the best decision.

Market innovation also includes staying focused on your marketing plan and approach. As your business grows, your marketing needs will shift and change. You may no longer need big, splashy ads to attract customers. Instead, you might want to use direct mail pieces to the mailing list you have established. Review your ads and marketing periodically, and add in new pieces to keep it fresh. Once you feel that you really are established, try something new with more narrow market aim. Consider hiring a professional to help you develop a full campaign. No matter what stage of business you are at, though, do not be tempted to eliminate marketing. Even though it seems to eat into the bottom line, it does pay your business back over time.

CASE STUDY: EXPAND WITH DEMAND

Lou Brown
Big Stone City, SD
www.lousgreenhouse.com

Lou Brown started his greenhouse business in the late 1960s. He and a neighbor constructed a 320-square-foot greenhouse on the side of a hill using lumber and plastic. A wood stove provided heat for the tender plants. They worked together again the second year, adding onto the greenhouse, but the third year Lou decided to go out on his own.

In 1969 he converted an old chicken brooding house into a greenhouse. At this point he considered building greenhouses as nothing more than a hobby. He did, however, have enough extra growing in his greenhouses that he started selling plants on the side. He quickly sold out of his plant stock so he decided to add onto the brooding house to increase his growing capacity. He had to make further additions each of the next three years to keep up with demand. By his fifth year of business he decided to construct a 24-foot by 60-foot greenhouse. Today, Brown has grown his business to include 17 greenhouses, ten Nexus® bays, and three portable hoop greenhouses.

As his nursery has grown, his need for labor has also increased. In 1973, Brown hired his first seasonal employee. In 1977 business had grown to the point that he needed 26 seasonal employees to help during the busy season of planting and selling. Today he employs 30 seasonal employees. Forty-four years after its humble start in a small brooding house, Brown's business has grown enormously. Today, he sells more than 1 million bedding and vegetable starter plants, 1,300 trees, and 2,500 shrubs annually. On a typical weekend, his greenhouse sees about 1,000 customers.

Brown's business strategy has been to only add onto his greenhouses and hire employees when he has reached the point where he sells out of stock — a great strategy for any small business. His suggestion for those interested in starting a greenhouse is to start small as a hobby and begin with vegetables as they are the easiest to grow. If one wants to grow flowers, large seeded flowers such as marigolds are easier to grow than small seeded flowers such as petunias and pansies.

Creating an Exit Strategy

Once you are past this stressful startup phase, you will settle into the routine and joy of farming. If all goes well, you will see profits and a growing business with great prospects. You truly will love your job and will not be able to imagine doing anything else. You surely do not want to think about ending it all, but the one certainty in business is that things are uncertain. Protecting yourself and your business with a well-thought-through exit plan is your insurance against uncertainty and the only way to preserve the business you have built up. Some changes you face might be desirable, such as selling your business, transferring ownership to a family member, or retirement. Other exits can be undesirable such as bankruptcy, forced liquidation, stoppage of work due to illness, or even unexpected death of a business principal. All of these changes can impact employees, your business as a whole, your tax obligations, and possibly your personal assets negatively. Planning for your exit, whether it is forced or expected, is a crucial element of every good business strategy. It is not something you need to dwell on — formulate your plans, file them away, and review periodically as your business changes.

An exit strategy dovetails perfectly with the efficient maintenance of your business. If you have handled and addressed the topics discussed in this book, your exit plan is just a matter of deciding how you want the future to look. Ultimately, you want to step down with a profitable, valuable business that allows you to leave with assets or money or hand off a business that will continue to thrive. Running things well with the bottom line in mind keeps this value high. Keeping good records, staying current with licensing and taxes, and maintaining a loyal customer base will make for a smooth and profitable transition with limited fees and taxes. Dealing with unexpected life changes requires keeping a current will specifically stating your intentions and maintaining adequate life, health, and disability insurance. Be sure to hire a family law or tax attorney to assist you in drawing up the necessary documents.

Legalities

A sole proprietorship is the only business structure that is easy to close, transfer, or liquidate. All other business structures require legal filings, permit or license transfers, tax implications, and even unemployment or retraining requirements. The rules for partnerships, limited liability corporations, and corporations require additional actions that are specific to each situation. Additionally, transferring ownership to a family member or taking a large profit from a sale can result in significant estate, gift, or capital gains taxes. The following sections briefly will describe your options but it is recommended to consult with an attorney specializing in each area. The SBA and SCORE websites also fully explain each topic and offer great tips on wading through the red tape. Rules and regulations vary by state and change with legislation, so be sure to check current information before proceeding with your exit plan.

Valuing your business

Before you can exit your business through succession, transfer, or sales, you must know the value of your business. Again, ongoing record keeping and business planning will make it much easier to determine the value. This value is consists of all the tangibles that make up your business including animals, buildings, land, equipment, patents, contracts, inventory, and so on. It also includes those things that are hard to put a number on such as customer base, brand loyalty, innovative potential, and market plans. Of course, you will need to value both the tangible and intangible to come to a fair price for both you and your buyer or successor. The best way to value your business is to hire an impartial appraiser skilled in farm appraisals and valuation. You then can use this number in your negotiations.

How you take payment is up to you and depends greatly on your before planning and future goals. You might be happy to hand over your business to your son or daughter completely with no expectation of money. You also might be willing to take shares in the future company as payment for the business. You might not want to sell the entire business but split it into two divisions, one of which you will keep. The possibilities are endless and depend on your situation. The one commonality in value and payment is that you must work with a professional to be sure you are receiving a fair settlement and that the transfer is made properly.

Succession planning

For many, passing on a successful business to a family member or business partner is the ultimate goal and measure of achievement. Making a smooth transition will ensure that the business you have built up will continue to thrive in capable hands. When done correctly, your customers barely will notice a change, and your successors will be confident in their new roles. In many cases, you can step down from day-to-day operations but stay involved as a consultant, shareholder, or board member. You can set up your succession with whatever structure works for you and those taking over the company. The SCORE website offers a thorough discussion on properly planning your succession and includes these five steps:

1.   Choosing a successor. The right person to take control might not be the most obvious person. Assess your choice as you would any

other partner. If your top choice seems to be not quite ready to take over, give yourself plenty of time to train him or her, and be prepared for a slower exit.

2. Training. Allow your chosen successor to shadow you and other key business principals so he or she can learn all aspects of the business. Be sure to introduce your successor to your advisers, your suppliers, and your customers.

3. Set a timetable. Set clear deadlines for training goals and transfer of responsibility. This helps both of you understand your role in the company, provides stability for employees, and defines who should be making decisions.

4. Prepare yourself. After working for so many years, it will be hard to not be involved in the company. Shorten your work days gradually, and allow the power to transition to your successor.

5. Leave. This will be the hardest part but you must step aside and let your business grow under the new regime. Enjoy the retirement you have worked so hard to achieve.

Obviously, succession due to death or illness will not go this smoothly. You can however, choose a successor and train him or her in as much as possible. So often, a successful business fails, and the family suffers unnecessary hardship because things are left in disarray when a business owner dies. By planning ahead for this unexpected event, you will not only give your family a profitable business to help financially but you also will relieve them from the stress of making these decisions. Talk with your attorney to draw up a will and right of succession for your business.

Transferring ownership or selling your business

Transferring ownership or selling your business is similar to succession planning but is more of a clean break in which you can walk away with profits and will no longer be involved in the business. The transfer or sale can be made to a family member, a stranger, or to a business partner, and owners have several options for transferring ownership rights. These options include:

- Outright sale. In this scenario, you sell all the assets, inventory, customer base, name, and brand in full, receive payment immediately, and cease to be involved in the business.

- Gradual sale. Similar to stepping down through succession, a gradual sale allows you to transfer business ownership, receive monthly income from this sale, and still remain involved in the business. Of course, you basically will become an employee and no longer have decision-making powers. This option helps buyers who cannot afford an outright sale or who need assistance in learning the business.

- Lease agreement. This arrangement allows you to step away temporarily from the business. By transferring your business ownership through a lease, you commit to a contract that details the conditions, terms, and payments you will receive for these temporary rights. Be sure the person you are leasing to will maintain the business to your standards.

In all cases, the best way to proceed with a sale or transfer is to prepare a sales agreement. This should contain all terms of the purchase and is best drawn up by a broker and reviewed by an attorney. This agreement defines everything that you intend to sell including the specifics of the business, assets, customer lists, intellectual property rights, and more. Visit the SBA website for a sample sales agreement.

Closing the business

The time might come when you need to make the tough decision of shutting your business down. Situations in your life might be changing and ending your business is not necessarily considered a failure. In addition to the legal and tax requirements of closing a business down, you must take steps to protect your own assets and reputation. You truly do not want to burn bridges or damage the goodwill you have built in the community or with other farmers.

If you decide it is time to be done, end your business in a professional manner, and be sure to honor all the commitments you have made in promised products, payments, or contracts. If you cannot fulfill your obligations, give your customers plenty of advance notice or offer to help them find an alternative. By ending your relationship in this way, you will keep the door open if you decide to re-open your business. Follow up your closure with a heartfelt thank you to all your good customers and suppliers. Remember to delete or change any website links, phone numbers, or advertising pieces currently running in the market. Keep all your records for three to five years and continue to file necessary business taxes for the year.

After closing and paying all your bills, you might find yourself with un-wanted inventory and assets. There are multiple ways to liquidate these assets. You can sell the entire farm as a whole — if the new owner is planning on running it as a farm, though, it would be best to sell it as an up-and-running business. You can have an on-site auction or sell your assets through an online auction service or classifieds sites. You also can donate equipment, seed, animals, or land to a worthy charity or nonprofit, such as your local school or community college.

Additional exit issues

Many more complex and industry-specific issues are wrapped up in the end of a business, and these are best studied separately through books or websites written on the subject. You have a lot of options beyond those discussed in this chapter, and these include taking your business public, merging with another company, developing a franchise arrangement, or pursuing bankruptcy. Every single option entails legalities, tax implications, contracts, and negotiations. Some of these selections can take years to complete and have the potential to affect your entire financial future negatively. Research the SBA website for more details, and talk with your team of advisers for more information.

Conclusion

❦

Farming is an adventure into many fields. Not only do you need skills in everything farm-related, but you also must navigate the fields of marketing, customer service, taxes, laws, government assistance, banking, and more. And through it all you, must keep one eye on the bottom line and the other on your future. After reading this book, you might be a bit overwhelmed by all that is required to get your farm up and running. Do not despair just yet, take one step at a time, tackle each challenge as it comes, and eventually, you will be an experienced, successful farmer and businessperson. Remember that your journey is part of the adventure, and relish each new skill as you acquire it. Who knows, you might find that you have extraordinary marketing skills or fantastic financial negotiation ability.

While farming might seem to be an isolated profession, your daily life will bring you into contact with a wide range of people. Use each of these encounters to your advantage and build a network of trusted friends and advisers. Your landlord or seed supplier can answer tough questions, your customers can help you find areas for growth, and even your competition might be willing to team up for a joint venture. Opportunities really are sprouting all around you as long as you are willing to look, learn, and listen.

Years from now you will look back on this time as an exhilarating experience and treasure even the difficulties you faced as a new farmer. With time behind you and your farm spread out before you, you will know it was all worth it.

Thank you for letting me share your dreams and guide you into the adventure. I sincerely hope this book has helped you take that first step into a life of farming and wish you good growing conditions, healthy animals, fertile soil, and successful selling. Happy farming!

Appendix A

Sample Documents and Worksheets

❦

Marketing worksheet

Describe your potential customer.

_____

_____

Who are your competitors?

_____

_____

How can you compete in this market?

_____

_____

What are your strengths and weaknesses in comparison to competitors?

_____

_____

What can you do better than your competitors?

_____

_____

Are there any governmental or legal factors affecting your business?

_____

_____

What advantages does your product have over the competition?

_____

_____

What type of image do you want for your product?

_____

_____

What features will be emphasized?

_____

_____

What is your pricing strategy?

_____

_____

Is your pricing in line with your image?

_____

_____

Do your prices properly cover costs?

_____

_____

What types of promotion will you use? (Examples include using television, radio, direct mail, personal contacts, newspapers, magazines, yellow pages, billboards, the Internet, classifieds, and trade associations)

_____

_____

Sample Articles of Organization for a Florida LLC

ARTICLE I - Name
The name and purpose of the Limited Liability Company is:

Fictitious Name International Trading Company, LLC
Purpose: To conduct...

ARTICLE II - Address
The mailing address and street address of the principal office of the Limited Liability Company is:

Street Address: 1234 International Trade Drive
             Beautiful City, FL 33003

Mailing Address: P.O. Box 1235
             Beautiful City, FL 33003

**ARTICLE III - Registered Agent, Registered Office,
and Registered Agent's Signature**
The name and the Florida street address of the registered agent are:

    John Doe
    5678 New Company Lane
    Beautiful City, FL 33003

Having been named as registered agent and to accept service of process for the above stated Limited Liability Company at the place designated in this certificate, I hereby accept the appointment as registered agent and agree to act in this capacity. I further agree to comply with the provisions of all statutes relating to the proper and complete performance of my duties, and I am familiar with and accept the obligations of my position as a registered agent as provided for in Chapter 608, Florida Statutes.

Registered Agent's Signature

ARTICLE IV - Manager(s) or Managing Member(s)

<u>Title</u>   <u>Name & Address</u>
"MGR" = Manager
"MGRM" = Managing Member

MGR   Jane Doe
              234 Manager Street
              Beautiful City, FL 33003

MGRM   Jim Unknown
              789 Managing Member Drive
              Beautiful City, FL 33003

ARTICLE V - Effective Date

The effective date of this Florida Limited Liability Company
shall be January 1, 2014.

REQUIRED SIGNATURE:

_____

Signature of a member or an authorized representative of a member

Sample Articles of Incorporation for Alabama

STATE OF ALABAMA
DOMESTIC FOR-PROFIT CORPORATION
ARTICLES OF INCORPORATION GUIDELINES

INSTRUCTIONS:

STEP 1: CONTACT THE OFFICE OF THE SECRETARY OF STATE AT (334) 242-5324 TO RESERVE A CORPORATE NAME.

STEP 2: TO INCORPORATE, FILE THE ORIGINAL, TWO COPIES OF THE ARTICLES OF INCORPORATION, AND THE CERTIFI-CATE OF NAME.

RESERVATION IN THE COUNTY WHERE THE CORPORA-TION'S REGISTERED OFFICE IS LOCATED. THE SECRETARY OF STATE'S FILING FEE IS $40. PLEASE CONTACT THE JUDGE OF PROBATE TO VERIFY FILING FEES.

PURSUANT TO THE PROVISIONS OF THE ALABAMA BUSINESS CORPORATION ACT, THE UNDERSIGNED HEREBY ADOPTS THE FOLLOWING ARTICLES OF INCORPORATION.

Article I. The name of the corporation:

Article II. The duration of the corporation is "perpetual" unless otherwise stated.

Article III. The corporation has been organized for the following purpose(s):

Article IV. The number of shares, which the corporation shall have the authority to issue, is_____.

Article V. The street address (NO P.O. BOX) of the registered office:

_____

_____, and the

name of the registered agent at that office:

_____.

Article VI. The name(s) and address(es) of the Director(s):

Article VII. The name(s) and address(es) of the Incorporator(s):

Type or Print Name of Incorporator

_____

Signature of Incorporator

_____

Rev. 7/03

Any provision that is not inconsistent with the law for the regulation of the internal affairs of the corporation or for the restriction of the transfer of shares may be added.

IN WITNESS THEREOF, the undersigned incorporator executed these Articles of Incorporation on this the _____ day of _____, 20_____.

Printed Name and Business Address of Person Preparing this Document:

Sample cash-flow worksheet

A.D. Farmer

Cash-Flow Projection

January 1, 2014 to December 31, 2014

CASH TRANSACTION MONTH   1 2 3 4 5 6 7 8 9 10 11 12

Beginning Cash

Add Receipts:

    Sales

    Loan proceeds

    Contributions

Total Receipts

Total Cash Flow

Less Disbursements:

    Labor

    Feed

    Fertilizer & chemicals

    Seed

    Utilities

    Interest on loans

    Gas and oil

    Repairs

    Cattle purchases

    Advertising

    Loan payment

    Capital purchases

    Living expenses

Total Disbursements

Total Cash Outflow

NET CASH FLOW

Sample balance sheet

A.D. Farmer

Balance Sheet

on January 1, 2014

ASSETS

Current Assets

Cash in bank

Accounts receivable

Inventory

Total Current Assets

Fixed Assets

Land

Buildings (less depreciation)

Machinery (less depreciation)

Total Fixed Assets

TOTAL ASSETS

LIABILITIES

Current Liabilities

Accounts payable

Short-term loans

Other payments due within one year

Total Current Liabilities

Long-Term Liabilities

Long-term loans

Farm mortgages

Total long-term liabilities

OWNER'S EQUITY

TOTAL LIABILITIES & EQUITY

Sample income and expense statement

A.D. Farmer

Income and Expense Statement

January 1, 2014 to December 31, 2014

INCOME Total Percentage of Total Income

Sales 450,000

Total Income 450,000

VARIABLE EXPENSES

Wages 50,000

Feed 125,000

Crop Expenses 45,000

Gas and Oil 23,000

Maintenance 6,000

Total Variable Expenses 249,000

CONTRIBUTION MARGIN 201,000

FIXED EXPENSES

Depreciation 35,000

Insurance 4,000

Rent 55,000

Property tax 3,000

Interest 44,000

Total Fixed Expenses 141,000

NET INCOME 60,000

Appendix B

Helpful Websites

No. 1 best site to start with and find most everything you need — the Small Business Administration (**www.sba.gov**)

Community supported agriculture (CSA) — North Carolina Cooperative Extension website for Growing Small Farms (**www.ces.ncsu.edu/chatham/ag/SustAg/csaguide.html**)

Consumer protection — Better Business Bureau (**www.bbb.org**), Chamber of Commerce (**www.chamberofcommerce.com**)

Cooperative business management — Stronger Together Cooperative (**www.strongertogether.coop**)

Credit card readers — **squareup.com** or **payanywhere.com**

Credit scores and ranking — **www.equifax.com**

Crowd funding — **www.fquare.com**, **www.kickstarter.com**, **www.circleup.com**, **www.rockthepost.com**

Farmer's Almanac, P.O. Box 1609, Lewiston, Maine 04240 (**www.farmersalmanac.com**)

Farm banks — American Bankers Association (ABA) (**www.aba.com**), Farm Credit Administration (**www.fca.gov**), Farm Credit System lenders search by county (**www.farmcreditnetwork.com**), Farm Credit Council (**www.fccouncil.com**)

Farm life, general advice — *Grit magazine,* Ogden Publications, Inc., 1503 SW 42nd St. Topeka, Kansas 66609-1265 (**www.grit.com**)

Food safety — **www.foodsafety.gov**

Franchising your business — International Franchise Association (**www.franchise.org**)

General gardening — National Gardening Association (**www.garden.org**)

Grants, private — Foundation Center (**www.foundationcenter.org**)

Grants, governmental — **www.grants.gov**

Heritage seed suppliers — Seed Savers Exchange (**www.seedsavers.org**)

Livestock selection and animal raising — Ontario County's Finger Lakes area Agriculture (**www.fingerlakesagriculture.com/involved/livestock.php**)

Online banking — PayPal (**www.paypal.com**), Quicken Loans (**www.quickenloans.com**)

Online sales and listings — LocalHarvest (**www.localharvest.com**), eBay (**www.ebay.com**), Etsy (**www.etsy.com**), craigslist (**www.craigslist.org**)

Mentoring and education — SCORE (**www.score.org**)

Peer-to-peer lending — Prosper (**www.prosper.com**), Lending Club (**www.lendingclub.com**)

Pigs and hogs — Ontario County Agricultural Enhancement Board (**www.fingerlakesagriculture.com**)

Postharvest care — Postharvest Technology Research Center at University of California, Davis (**postharvest.ucdavis.edu**)

Rotational grazing methods — University of Wisconsin Extension Service, Learning Store (**www.learningstore.uwex.cdu/assets/pdfs/ A3529.pdf**)

Sheep and goats — University of Maryland's Small Ruminant Page (**www.sheepandgoat.com**)

Small business lobbying and advocacy group — The S Corporation Association of America (**www.s-corp.org**)

Small farms general info — *Hobby Farms* (**www.hobbyfarms.com**), *Mother Earth News* (**www.motherearthnews.com**), *Grit* (**www.grit.com**)

Small farms guide — University of Minnesota Extension Service, Small Farms Information (**www1.extension.umn.edu/food/ small-farms**)

Trademarks and patents — United States Patent and Trademark Office (USPTO) (**www.uspto.gov**)

Vehicle licensing and road restrictions — Department of Transportation, Federal Motor Carrier Safety Administrations (DOT, FMCSA): (**www.fcsma.dot.gov**)

USDA National Organic Program (**www.ams.usda.gov**)

USDA Risk Management Agency (RMA) (**www.rma.usda.gov**)

Appendix C

Government Acronym Cheat Sheet

AFSIC: Alternative Farming Systems Information Center

AMS: Agricultural Marketing Service

ATTRA: The National Sustainable Agriculture Information Service

CDL: Commercial Drivers License

DNR: Department of Natural Resources

DOT: Department of Transportation,

EPA: Environmental Protection Agency

EQIP: Environmental Quality Incentives Program

FCA: Farm Credit Administration

FCIC: Federal Crop Insurance Corporation

FDIC: Federal Deposit Insurance Corporation

FICA: Federal Insurance Contributions Act (aka Social Security)

FMCSA: Federal Motor Carrier Safety Administrations

FMPP: Farmers Market Promotion Program

FSA: Farm Service Agency

FSIS: Food Safety and Inspection Service

GVWR: Gross Vehicle Weight Rating

IRS: Internal Revenue Service

NAL: National Agricultural Library

NCAT: National Center for Appropriate Technology

NCUSIF: National Credit Union Share Insurance Fund

NIFA: Cooperative Extension System and National Institute of Food and Agriculture

NOP: National Organic Program

NRCS: Natural Resources Conservation Service

RMA: Risk Management Agency

SARE: Sustainable Agriculture Research and Education Outreach

SBA: Small Business Administration

SNAP: Supplemental Nutrition Assistance Program

SWCD: Soil and Water Conservation District

USDA: United States Department of Agriculture

USPTO: United States Patent and Trademark Office

Bibliography

❧❦❧

Adam, Katherine L. *Community Supported Agriculture.*
www.attra.org, 2006.

Averkamp, Harold. *What are sales taxes?*
www.blog.accountingcoach.com, 2011.

Chadwick, Janet. *The Beginner's Guide to Preserving Food at Home.*
North Adams, Massachusetts: Storey Publishing, 2009.

Coleman, Eliot. *The New Organic Gardener's Four-Season Harvest.*
Post Mills, Vermont: Chelsea Green Publishing Company, 1992.

Holthaus, Gary. *From the Farm to the Table.* Lexington, Kentucky:
University Press of Kentucky, 2006.

Kerr, Graham. *Growing at the speed of life: a year in the life
of my first kitchen garden.* New York: Penguin, 2011.

Kivirist, Lisa. *8 Tips for Beginning Farmers' Market Vendors.*
www.hobbyfarms.com, 2012.

Lancaster, Adelaide, and Amy Abrams. *The Big Enough Company.* New York: Penguin Group, 2011.

Levatino, Michael and Audrey. *The Joy of Hobby Farming.* New York: Skyhorse Publishing, 2011.

Madigan, Carleen, ed. *The Backyard Homestead.* North Adams, Massachusetts: Storey Publishing, 2009.

Markham, Brett. *Maximizing your Mini Farm.* New York: Skyhorse Publishing, 2012.

Pakroo, Peri. *The Small Business Start-Up Kit.* Nolo, 2012.

Pleasant, Barbara. *Starter vegetable gardens: 24 no-fail plans for small organic gardens.* North Adams, Massachusetts: Storey Publishing, 2010.

Ramberg, JJ, Lisa Everson, and Frank Silverstein. *It's Your Business.* Business Plus, 2012.

Roza, Greg. Great *Networking Skills.* New York: The Rosen Publishing Group, 2008.

Cold Storage for Fruits & Vegetables. North Adams, Massachusetts: Storey Publishing, 1988.

Time Life How-To Series. *Yard & Garden Projects: Easy, Step-By-Step Plans and Designs for Beautiful Outdoor Spaces. Time-Life* Books, 1998.

Steingold, Fred. *The Complete Guide to Selling a Business.* Nolo, 2012.

Author Biographies

Dr. Melissa Nelson is a graduate of the University Of Minnesota — College Of Veterinary Medicine. She currently lives on a beef cattle farm near Ortonville, Minnesota.

Julie Fryer lives in a small farming community in southeastern Minnesota with her husband and two sons. When she's not writing, Julie can be found in her large vegetable and flower gardens, scouring farmers' markets and country auctions, or in the kitchen preserving her bounty. She is the author of several how-to books and articles including *The Complete Guide to Your New Root Cellar* and *The Teen's Ultimate Guide to Making Money When You Can't Find a Job.*

Index